THE LOUISIANA CATAHOULA
LEOPARD DOG

by

DON ABNEY

Doral Publishing, Inc.

Wilsonville, Oregon

1996

D1214122

Published by Doral Publishing, Inc., 8560 SW Salish Lane #300, Wilsonville
OR 97070-9612. Order through Login Publishers Consortium, Chicago IL.

Printed in the United States of America.

Edited by Luana Luther.
Cover by Mary Jung.

Library of Congress Number: 95-83697
ISBN: 0-944875-44-0

Abney, Don.
   The Louisiana catahoula leopard dog / by
Don Abney. -- Wilsonville, Or. : Doral Pub.,
c1996.

   p. : ill. ; cm.

   Includes bibliographical references and
index.
   ISBN: 0-944875-44-0

   1. Louisiana catahoula. 2. Hounds.   I.
Title.

SF429.L   636.75'3 dc20
                              95-83697

To my wife Kathleen.

Thanks for the understanding

and for all that you have done.

Acknowledgments

Without the help and input from the following list of people, this book would not have been possible. Thank you one and all.

Kathleen B. Abney, wife and partner

Aubrey & Elaine Aden, Aden Catahoulas, Carriere, Mississippi

Bob & Janette Blair, Blair's T/O Catahoulas, Wills Point, Texas

Diane Bordelon, Library Reference Department Head, Lobby Branch, Jefferson Parish Public Library

Mrs. J.S. (Betty Ann) Eaves, President, National Association of Louisiana Catahoulas and Author of the Louisiana Catahoula Collection

Phil & Kathy Grady, Catahoula breeders, Seven Springs, North Carolina

James (Pete) Hendry, DVM, General Animal Hospital, Covington, Louisiana

Amos & Susan Mann, Two Diamond Catahoulas, Wills Point, Texas

Dr. George Strain, Ph.D., Director, Louisiana State University, Veterinary Medicine, Baton Rouge, Louisiana

Vernon Traxler Jr. and family, Abita Springs, Louisiana

INTRODUCTION

The decision to write a book about the Louisiana Catahoula came after I received numerous telephone calls and letters from people asking me what a Catahoula was and could I describe one to them. These inquiries, along with some encouragement from Mr. Vernon Traxler and his wife Rita, gave me the incentive. Little did I know that what I would be writing would become contradictory to what had been handed down for generations.

Information about the dog's accomplishments and abilities were relatively simple to obtain. All I had to do was talk to a few owners and breeders who were using their dogs for various purposes and write it down. Since I am a breeder and trainer who knows quite a few of these owners, I thought it would be simple for me to write the uses of the Catahoula. This is where simple ended.

The trouble started when I went to work researching the history of the Catahoula. At first, the origin of the Catahoula was vague. I could not find any mention in any of the history books. I found various magazine articles written about them and the legend that had been handed down over the years, but that was all. When I got deeper into Louisiana history, the contradictions started. It was only after numerous visits to various libraries and many hours of research that I came to the conclusions you are about to read.

It is not my intention to discredit any of the works of others prior to this writing. What is written in this book is the belief of the author to be what transpired in the creation of the Catahoula. It is my intention to provide factual information about the Catahoula so that this breed does not suffer ruination at the hands of uninformed persons. I would also like to encourage owners and breeders alike to attend shows and display their animals.

If, after reading this book, you still have questions that you feel need to be answered, you may write to me at POB 248, Abita Springs, LA 70420. I will gladly answer your questions.

Regardless of whether or not your beliefs differ from mine, one thing is certain. There are only a few breeds of dogs that have the distinct honor of being created in the United States.

One of them is the Louisiana Catahoula Leopard Dog.

TABLE OF CONTENTS

Chapter 1

HISTORY

After spending countless hours in libraries throughout Louisiana searching through old records and history books, I believe the following transpired in the creation of the Louisiana Catahoula Leopard Dog.

To help you understand how I came to this conclusion, I have included some of Louisiana's history and history on the Indians of the area. These are the events that took place.

On May 30, 1539, Hernando de Soto reached the shores of the New World somewhere around Charlotte Bay, Florida, in search of gold and treasure. With enough supplies for himself and 1000 men, a herd of pigs, and what has been referred to as "war dogs," De Soto began his expedition across what is now the southernmost part of the United States. In some history books, there is reference to the Spaniards using bloodhounds. This reference was a slang term describing the blood-thirsty dogs that were used and not the species of dog we know as the Bloodhound. The war dogs, or bloodhounds, used by the Spaniards are believed to have been the Mastiff and the Greyhound. Laurel Drew, an historian of the Greyhound, traced the Greyhound and Mastiff accompanying Spanish explorers in the 1500s. The Mastiffs were used as dual-purpose dogs. During battles, the dogs would be turned loose to assist in the fighting. At night, the dogs would be placed around the perimeter of the camp to guard their masters while they slept. Greyhounds were used as hunting dogs—assisting in the hunting and running down of small game.

De Soto traveled through Florida, Georgia, the Carolinas, Tennessee, Alabama, Mississippi and Louisiana. During his quest for gold and wealth, he encountered many Indian tribes. In his attempts to convert the Indians to his form of Christianity and to learn of their treasures, De Soto would use the war dogs to hunt, guard, intimidate and punish the Indians. One of his punishments involved chaining his prisoners to trees and allowing the dogs to tear them to pieces in full view of his other captives. This way he hoped to gain the respect of the Indians so they would tell him where he could find treasures and guide him through the new land. In October 1540, near Mobile Bay, Alabama, the expedition was attacked by an Indian army and narrowly escaped disaster.

De Soto, determined to find wealth, forged ahead, and, in the spring of 1541, discovered the Mississippi River. After crossing the river into Louisiana, he encountered another tribe of Indians of the Natchez nation. Some of the tribes of the Natchez nation were the Natchez, Tensas and Avoyelle. These are not all the tribes of the Natchez nation, but they are the ones of most importance to our story. The language of the Natchez nation was Muskhogean. Although the language of each tribe was the same, dialects were different. This sometimes led to confusion for the white man's understanding of exactly what was being said.

After arriving in Louisiana, De Soto first went north, where he met the Quizquiz Indians. This was a massive tribe that De Soto knew he would not be able to conquer as he had the other tribes. Instead, he made an attempt to gain the trust of this tribe. When he felt the time was right, he took the jewels from their idols. This made the Indians very angry, and, after being attacked and beaten back, De Soto decided to turn southward. The Quizquiz followed De Soto but encountered a rival tribe of Yazoo Indians. This time, the Quizquiz suffered defeat at the hands of their enemy. The surviving Quizquiz moved southward in search of De Soto and became known as the Tunica Indians.

On his journey southward, De Soto encountered another ferocious and mobile tribe known as the Tensas. This tribe did not hesitate in at-

Abney's Ladyhawke, NALC's first registered Catahoula to receive a Service Champion Award in Search and Rescue.

tacking the strange people in their land. Again, De Soto and his men took a beating.

Continuing southward, he came upon a tribe of friendly Indians known as the Avoyelles. No one knows why the Avoyelles took De Soto and his men into their village. They cared for the wounded and sick men until De Soto decided to leave the village. When they were able to travel, they left behind their sick and wounded animals. De Soto returned to the river near what was to become Jonesville, Louisiana, where he died of fever in 1542. He was buried in full body armor in the Mississippi River so the Indians would not know of his death or where his body had been laid to rest. This was done so that Indian enemies could not desecrate his grave. The 300 remaining men traveled down the Mississippi River and eventually returned to their homeland.

The Indians, never having seen dogs used the way they had been used against them, sought out the sick and wounded animals and nursed them back to health.

It is known that the fox will not mate with a dog, and the coyote was not present in Louisiana during this time. However, red wolves roamed in central Louisiana. They were known to stay near the Indian villages where they could scavenge food and they often became pets of the Indians. Some historians believe that the war dogs, Mastiff and Greyhound, were crossed with the red wolf. Being allowed to run free, these dogs bred and interbred among themselves. The result of this happenstance breeding is the wolf-dog that is mentioned in history books.

In 1682, Rene Robert Cavelier, Sieur de La Salle, accompanied by his chief lieutenant, Henri de Tonti, traveled down the Mississippi River to claim the valley for France. They named it Louisiana.

In 1684, La Salle returned to colonize the area, but his expedition met with many disasters.

In 1699, Pierre Lemoyne, Sieur d'Iberville, on an expedition from France, reached the mouth of the Mississippi and explored it to the Red River.

In 1700, Tonti joined the French settlers at the mouth of the Mississippi River and told stories of seeing strange-looking wolf-dogs with white eyes and mottled coats. After approximately 150 years of breeding free in the wild, the strange-looking dogs with the haunting glass eyes were discovered by the first white settlers.

Hearing of the abundance of wild game in the swamp lands, the French brought their own dogs with them to the New World. These dogs

Two Diamond's Job, owned by Amos and Susan Mann. Job is an NALC Show Champion.

were known as the *Berger De Beauce* or *Bas Rouge*. Today, this same dog is known as the Beauceron (pronounced bo-sher-on). It originated in Le Beauce, France, and was known to exist in 1578. These dogs were used in France for hunting wild boar. They were ferocious dogs and needed a strong hand. They were used to protect the French from the attacks of the Indians. Later on, through selective breeding, this breed became less aggressive and was trained as a herding dog.

In 1714, the first permanent settlement was established at Fort St. Jean Baptiste, now Natchitoches (pronounced nack-uh-tish). Not far from the fort was the village of the Avoyelle Indians. This was the same tribe of Indians that had cared for De Soto, and they showed no objection to the new people.

In 1729, the Natchez Indians rebelled against the French settlers in Mississippi, destroying Fort Rosalie. The French retaliated with a bloody vengeance in both Mississippi and Louisiana by killing and driving the Indians north. On January 25, 1733, the French under Bienville, exterminated the Natchez Indians.

Only a handful of Indian tribes remained in Louisiana, and they joined together in one village at the mouth of the Red River. These tribes were the Avoyelle, Tunica, Ofo, and Choctaw. They lived here without interference from the French.

Although the Catahoula is not mentioned by name during this time, references were made to the Indians using a "large wolf-like breed of dog" on their hunting trips. Learning how the Indians used the dogs to hunt game in the swamp, the settlers tried to use them for herding their cattle.

They found that the webbed feet of these dogs allowed them to go into the swamp and easily retrieve cattle that would normally have been lost.

It is my belief that the Beauceron was introduced to the wolf-like dog of the Indians in an attempt to create an even better dog able to work in the swamps. This would explain why some reddish black dogs with loud red trim will appear in a litter of all blue Leopard Catahoulas. It would also explain why the hound look is so prominent in the Catahoula.

The word *Catahoula* is said to be a Choctaw word that means "clear water." However, H.B. Cushman gives a different explanation of the Choctaw language in his book, *The History of Choctaw, Chickasaw and the Natchez Indians*, published in 1899. He explains that the word

Aden's Mariah insists that this cow move.

Catahoula was originally "kawahchula." This is an ancient Choctaw word meaning "barking fox." There are those who say the word Catahoula came from the Choctaw word "okatahulo," meaning "beloved lake." Again research shows that there was no such word in the Choctaw language. The word for "beloved lake" or "clear water" is "okhuata holitopa."

The relationship of "clear water" to "beloved lake" is purely speculation and interpretation of meaning. The Indian word for Choctaw is Couthaougoula (pronounced Coot-ha-oo-goo-la). Here is where I believe the French attempted to pronounce the Indian word Couthaougoula and transformed the word into "Catahoula." The reference to Catahoula Indians was a means of describing all the Indians in the area. Reference to the dog as a Catahoula was done as a mockery or slur toward the Indians. The inference was that the Indians were nothing more than dogs.

By 1805, only a handful of Avoyelles Indians remained. Again, the name Avoyelles is a French composition. Originally, the tribe was known as Avoy. The French pronounced it Avoyel then spelled it Avoyelle. All three spellings are found at different periods in history by different writers. This lead to confusion by readers not aware that all three spellings of the name refer to the same tribe of Indians.

There are some old stories that maintain that the Catahoula Indians lived at the mouth of the Red River and along its banks; however, there is no reference to Catahoula Indians in any of the history books. Unless we accept the French misinterpretation and pronunciation of the Indian word Couthaougoulas, the origin of the word Catahoula will remain a mystery.

Around 1930, George Traxler moved from Brandon, Mississippi, to live at Lake Providence, Louisiana. His wife was half Indian and half French. When talking with the Indians about their dogs and where they came from, the answer was always the same: "The dogs came with the white man from the east."

I am told that as late as 1950, the Catahoula Indians could be found living at the junction of the Red, Black, and Little Rivers in Catahoula parish, just to the southwest of Jonesville, Louisiana.

There are references to the Catahoula dog throughout the 1800s when the Bowie brothers, Jim and Rezin, owned some of them. It was said that Rezin Bowie, maker of the famous Bowie knife, would sleep with a Catahoula at his feet.

In the early 1900s, President Theodore Roosevelt came to Louisiana on a hunting trip and was introduced to a pair of Catahoulas. It was on this trip that the president refused to shoot a Louisiana Black Bear, thereby giving birth to a stuffed animal that would become known as the "Teddy Bear."

Even as early as the 1940s, the Catahoula was a little-known dog anywhere except by Louisiana hunters and farmers. The unique ability of this dog to hunt and herd, especially in the swamplands of Louisiana, made it the dog of choice for many. The Catahoula was prized for his ability to wind or air scent its prey. No matter where the livestock or game had wandered, you could bet the Catahoula would pick up its scent and bring it back. In most cases, the only way you got to own a Catahoula was if someone gave one to you. These dogs were not for sale.

This custom came from the 18th verse of 23 Deuteronomy that stated: "Thou shalt not bring the hire of a whore, or the price of a dog into the house..." Owners of these dogs would lease their dogs to other farmers for a time, but they would not sell the dogs. When puppies were born, they were used to replace dogs who were injured or killed during roundup. Only a few were given away.

No one knows for sure how the first Catahoula left Louisiana, but today there are Catahoulas in Canada, Brazil, the Virgin Islands, Mexico, Europe and in every state in the United States. Yet, there are those who have lived in Louisiana all their lives and do not know what a Catahoula is or what one even looks like.

I constantly receive requests by phone and mail asking me to describe the Catahoula. Well, that's kind of hard, since no two look exactly alike.

Governor Earl K. Long had an interest in the Catahoula and began collecting them on his travels around the state. These dogs were sent to Louisiana State Police Headquarters and Angola State Prison, where they were kept and used as stock patrol dogs. After his death, the dogs were almost forgotten, but a gentleman named Kline Rushing, a State Trooper and owner of Catahoulas, had a dream of making the Catahoula known. He and people who knew of their unique ability to get around in the Louisiana swampland pulled together in an attempt to save this unique breed. Mr. Rushing kept records of his matings, as did Mr. Vernon Traxler Jr., the grandson of George Traxler, as well as other breeders dedicated to saving the Catahoula.

Wolf River's Eli, owned by Janette Blair and shown by Nicole Mills.

I personally did not know Mr. Rushing, but I have become friends with Mr. Vernon Traxler. He is responsible for my becoming a breeder of Catahoulas and prompting me into this writing.

When Kline Rushing died in June 1977, his daughter, Ms. J. S. (Betty Ann) Eaves, with the help and support of some friends and family, took up his quest. It is because of her efforts that the Louisiana Catahoula has attained its present status. Collecting records from independent owners and compiling a method of tracking various matings, Ms. Eaves has successfully established the official registry for the Catahoula.

The National Association of Louisiana Catahoulas (NALC) became incorporated as a non-profit organization (with no paid officers) on October 10, 1977. Ms. Eaves is the president of this organization. The main function of the organization is to register only purebred Catahoulas. This is done by keeping a record of registration certificates, owners, and litter registrations. The official standard was established in 1984 from the input of NALC's Certified Breeders. This was an important factor in determining judging and breeding of Catahoulas.

Through her efforts, which she relates in her book, *The Catahoula Collection*, Ms. Eaves worked to make the Catahoula the state dog. On July 9, 1979, Governor Edwin Edwards signed a bill making the Louisiana Catahoula Leopard Dog the State Dog of Louisiana.

Today, the Catahoula is being bred for a variety of uses outlined in this book. The thing to remember is that the Catahoula of today is being, or should be, bred according to the standard as set forth by the NALC. This standard should be followed when acquiring or breeding a Catahoula.

I believe the Catahoula has the spirit of the wolf, the speed of the Greyhound, the strength of the Mastiff and the assertiveness of the Beauceron. All this is piled into a loving, intelligent and loyal companion who wants nothing more than to please his master.

In some circles, the Catahoula is referred to as a Cur Dog. This is because the dog was called a Catahoula Cur before the official naming of the dog by Governor Edwards. The governor, in naming the Catahoula the state dog, dropped Cur from its name and added Leopard Dog because of its strange coat.

In researching the Catahoula origins, I found other dogs referred to as curs. *Webster's New World Dictionary* defines cur as "a dog of mixed breed; mongrel." There are other definitions, but this is the one that interests me most. The reference to cur appears to include any dog whose origin cannot be determined and who accomplishes the same feats. If we are honest with ourselves, all dogs were curs at some time or other. Any breed that has come into existence was a mixed breed at some point in its origin.

No matter which explanation you choose to believe to be true, whether it is the beautifully poetic background of chance or just plain folks doing what they thought would help in the performance of their chores, the Catahoula still reigns king in Louisiana. Ask any Catahoula owner what he thinks of this dog. You had better find yourself a place to sit, because you're going to be listening to the answer for a while. It doesn't make any difference if the dog works livestock, guards, hunts, or is just the family pet, you're going to hear what a fine outstanding dog he is.

Even though the name was changed in 1979, there still are people today who will walk up to me and say: "Hey, is that a cur dog?" I simply smile and answer politely: "Yes, sir, but we prefer to call them Leopard Dogs." Most often the reply will be: "Uh huh, I thought so, you can tell by them eyes."

Chapter 2

Curs

I have been asked time and again if all curs are related to one another. I would have to say that the possibility exists that they may be related in some way.

I have researched the origin of the Catahoula but not all of the dogs known as curs. I know that Catahoulas were taken from Louisiana and used in other areas of the country. I know that some of these Catahoulas were crossed with other breeds of dog in an attempt to achieve a predetermined result. There is also the possibility that the curs in those areas were developed through the same process as the Catahoula.

In each of those locations, Curs are known by a formal name but are still referred to as Curs. For example, there are the Mountain Cur, Leopard Treeing Cur, Yellow Cur, Black Mouth Cur, etc.

The Catahoula's origin is based on the fact that DeSoto brought Spanish war dogs with him to the United States and that the Indians crossed them with the red wolf in Louisiana.

The possibility exists that, during his travels from Florida across the southern states to Louisiana, these same dogs could have been bred with other species of wolves or the Indian pariah dogs of those areas creating a dog that is somewhat similar.

Many years have passed and numerous crosses with other breeds of dog have taken place to better the curs of each area in their desired skills. It could be assumed that all southern curs could be related far back in their genealogy to the dogs of DeSoto. Without researching each cur and its history of origin, it is almost impossible to determine if all curs are related.

Some say that cur is a reference to the curled tail. Most curs have a tail that will make a curl over the back forming what looks like a question mark. By shortening the word curl it becomes cur. There are still others who will tell you that the word cur is a reference to the dogs as cowardly because of the way they will charge and then retreat, causing the game or stock to follow. Then Webster steps in and calls the dog a "mongrel."

Being referred to as cur is not used the way Webster defines it. Curs could be placed in a category of their own, since they do the same type work of other breeds, only in their own fashion.

The information contained in this book will surely help cur owners, breeders and buyers to be better prepared for the dogs they will eventually call theirs.

The chapters on Purchasing, Breeding and Care and Maintenance could be applied to almost any breed of dog.

The one thing that I highly recommend is that the Catahoula or any other cur dog should NEVER be bred to a wolf. Since these dogs had their beginnings with the wolf, any wolf crossing would surely be disastrous. Introducing the wolf blood back into a breed descending so closely from the wolf would be like the rebirth of a wild animal.

Most Catahoulas, as well as curs, are very wary of strangers. This is a wolf trait. Domesticated as they are, these dogs are very assertive, and the introduction of even more wolf-like tendencies could lead to aggressive behavior that could not be controlled. This does not mean that the wolf's bloodline would be the root cause of any problems. It means that you wouldn't know what dormant genes would be awakened by the crossing of these two animals. The resulting behavior could be overly aggressive or extremely shy. Either of these could lead to a dog who would be very difficult to handle or train. Both shy and aggressive behaviors may also lead to biting problems.

Chapter 3

TRAITS

The Louisiana Catahoula Leopard Dog has been described by some as the most versatile dog in the world. He has been used for herding, hunting, showing, guarding, search-and-rescue, narcotic detecting and just plain companionship.

The Catahoula has an uncanny ability to adapt to almost any environment. He can be found all over the United States, as well as in Canada, Mexico, Brazil and the Virgin Islands.

Catahoulas are born with a natural desire to herd. When observing a litter playing, you can see this as well as the establishment of the pecking order. You may see them mouthing each other about the neck and ears, and, as the litter gets older and stronger, you will see the pups chasing each other. As the chase goes on, the pups will try to catch the leader by grabbing the fleshy part of his neck, the side of his face, or his ear. If they are successful, they will pull the leader to the ground. They will also try to catch the front or rear leg at the upper quarter to cause the lead pup to fall. In reality, this play is a sharpening of the skills that a Catahoula will use when working a wild hog or a herd of cattle.

By observing a five- to eight-week-old litter, you can determine which pups will probably be the best working dogs and which will make the best pets. Because of this ingrained instinct, it is not necessary for the parents of the pups to be trained for hunting or working. This is one trait that breeders respect and have not made any attempts to remove, thereby producing good hunting and working dogs naturally.

The Catahoula can track a scent not only from the ground but also by air currents. If the scent is detected in the air, the dog will leave the track on the ground, hold his head high in the air, and move directly toward that scent. Some refer to this as "wind-ing" or "air scenting."

These dogs do not stray very far. When hunting, they will return to the owner to ensure all is well. Not being a hunter myself, I have been told by most hunters that what they like most is that they do not have to spend days looking for their dogs when the hunt is over. Some say that if you place the dog's blanket on the ground where you started he will return to that spot, lie on his blanket and wait for your return.

His webbed feet allow him to walk easily through swampy areas, as well as over snow. This also makes for excellent swimmers. Most will swim so high in the water that their backs will be out of the water.

Temperament is one subject that always arises when speaking about Catahoulas. The Catahoula is at home with his family and will try his best to please his master. You will find that, once you have a Catahoula, it will be difficult to tell if you own the dog or if the dog owns you. When a Catahoula grows up with a child, you will find that the dog will protect that child no matter what. Even to his death. These dogs are very protective of what or whom they think they own.

In spite of this assertive nature, the Catahoula is a very controllable dog. He learns very rapidly what is right and what is wrong. I find that males tend to be more obnoxious than females, especially when other males are in the area. They want the pecking order, dominance, established immediately. As with most dogs, you have to prove to them that you are the leader of this pack (family). Once this is established, there should not be any problems of control. Children are sometimes annoyed with them when they are playing games such as hide and seek. The dog believes that the children are a part of his job and will try to herd them into a bunch. This is so that they will not become separated or lost. This

Ladyhawke, Shadow and Honey taking a dip. If there's water anywhere, a Catahoula will find it.

Aden's Pib, Pretty Boy and Mariah are all show champions who also work cattle.

Catahoulas in the house? Of course, if they are allowed to exercise first. Otherwise, they might eat your house.

Aden's Patchwork Pib, Rene's Doctor Luke and Aden's Pib's Angel work cattle and win in shows.

is not what children want when they are playing, but the Catahoula believes these are his and must be guarded.

Catahoulas are very wary of strangers. If you don't belong on his property, he is going to let you know. My home is about 250 feet off the road. There is a gravel drive leading up to the house. The kennel is about another 100 feet from the house and surrounded by trees. If anyone so much as walks on the gravel, every dog in the kennel starts barking. Talk about a burglar alarm! It is not only the movement of the gravel. I have had friends walk up to the fence at the side of the drive to talk to me, and the dogs started barking before I knew my friends were there.

The hair coat of the dogs is short to shorter. What does this mean? Well, some Catahoulas have a hair coat that is about the length of a Labrador Retriever. Others have hair that looks as if it's painted on their skin. I like to refer to this type coat as wash-and-wear.

A Catahoula is not always easy to keep clean. If there is water any-where, even a puddle, he is going to walk through it. This is when you really appreciate that short hair.

It is because of this short hair that heartworm prevention is a must. Catahoulas, like most short-haired dogs, are susceptible to heartworm. I strongly recommend that a preventative medication be used through-out the life of the dog.

The tail is usually held high in the air and will curl over the back as if in a question mark. When free to roam, after running around like crazy, you can see the tail held high over the back. If something gets his attention, he will freeze in a position looking in that particular direction. His ears will perk and the tail will make that question mark. When you call him to you, he will tuck his tail between his legs like a whipped pup. Some say it's a show of submission. I've seen dogs coming to their owners with their tails tucked between their legs and suddenly turn with the tails raised when something gets their attention.

Catahoulas have voracious appetites. They are not picky eaters. It is not necessary to dress up their food with enticements to get them to eat. If it's good food, they'll eat it.

These dogs are very disease resistant. In talking to other breeders, I have found that there is very little that affects the Catahoula. Heart-worm seems to be the biggest problem—and preventive treatments solve this problem.

Sgt. Joe Bernard and Don Abney discussing the Easter Parade at Picayune. Ms. Ladyhawke is wearing her work jacket.

This is a very hearty animal. In spite of the coward-appearing approach to his owner, this dog is hard to keep down. Even if a dog gets cut by a boar on a hunt, which sometimes happens, these dogs will want to continue the hunt the next day. Keeping a Catahoula down and calm can be a problem if ill. He will want to work or play just to please you. This is a very loyal animal.

The eyes of the Catahoula are as interesting as the dog's coat. Although the *glass* eyes (light blue) are the most sought after, eye color may vary. Some of these dogs will have amber (yellow or gold) eyes and others will have green or brown eyes. Then there are the ones that have a different color in each eye.

The light-blue-colored eyes of the Catahoula are not really a color at all. It is a lack of pigmentation that causes the eye to appear like glass. What you are actually seeing is the back of the eye. This is the reason the eye will show red when light hits it in the dark. You are actually seeing the blood vessels.

If you acquire a dog with glass eyes, be prepared to answer the following questions as long as the dog lives. "Is your dog blind?" "How come his eyes are a different color?" "What causes that?" I find the easiest answer to all those questions is: "Genetics."

Chapter 4

USES

Being referred to by his admirers as the most versatile dog in the world requires an explanation. I have tried to explain what these functions are and how the Catahoula goes about getting them done. Please understand that I do not engage in all of the activities performed by the Catahoula. The following explanations are from people engaged in those activities.

Breeders are often asked what the uses of the Catahoula are. The usual answer is work, hunt, show, guard and companionship. Now, not all breeders raise or train dogs for all of those purposes. It is possible, however, to pick a puppy for each of those categories from the same litter. How can that be? Who knows? That's just the way of a Catahoula.

Each puppy has in him the ability to work, hunt, show, guard or just be a pet. Just being pets is sometimes the hardest thing for Catahoulas. They are born with this innate ability to herd. Dogs that have never been around cattle will instinctively try to circle them when they are introduced.

Following are the things I know the Catahoula is capable of doing:

Work

Primarily, the Catahoula was used to round up hogs that were deep in the swampland of Louisiana. Since there are a lot of marshy areas in Louisiana, the Catahoula with his webbed feet and a desire to work made him the perfect dog for this terrain. If you haven't seen a Catahoula work a hog, you haven't seen anything. Sometimes called the coward dog because of the way he darts in and out at a hog, the Catahoula will tantalize the lead hog into chasing him. This chase may be only 10 feet, but the Catahoula will go back and aggravate his prey again and again. The lead hog will squeal during his ordeal, bringing the rest of the herd to his aid. This show will continue until he gets the entire herd to follow him into the pens. This could be a distance of yards or miles. When two or three dogs are used, one dog is the leader and the other two are the helpers. If the lead dog is working the herd by having it follow him, the other two will work the sides and rear, keeping it bunched and moving forward. The Catahoula thinks it's a game. Once the hogs are in the pen, the dog will go to a prearranged area at the back of the pen where he can jump up and over the fence.

When working cattle, the dogs must be taught either to drive or lead the herd. This is usually a matter of choice by the owner.

The dog will do either. Usually, two or three dogs are used when bringing a herd into the pens. The dogs are non-stop action. They will first bunch the herd together and keep it packed tightly, while they circle the herd and calm it down. Then the rancher will move in and start the cows moving. The lead dog will get in front of the herd and lead it in the direction the rancher desires. This is quite noisy and the barking rarely stops. If one of the cows decides that she isn't going to move, it's not beyond the notion of the Catahoula to jump up and bite her on the nose or ear. This usually gets her moving. All the while this is happening, the rancher is either on horseback or on foot giving directions to the dogs. If a cow breaks and runs, one of the dogs will go after her and bring her back to the herd. Again, the handler directs which dog he wishes to fetch up the cow. The two other dogs still keep the herd bunched and moving while the lead dog takes it to the pens. As the cows are brought into the pens, the dogs will have a place in the pen where they can get out. If a place were not provided for them to escape, they

Blair's Radar, owned by John Nicholson, demonstrates his ability to get out of the way.

Diamond Cutter and Cayenne Sue hold three hogs at bay.

Blair's Diamond Cutter and Cayenne Sue, owned by Amos Mann. As one dog is pursued, the other dog intercepts the hog. A fine working pair.

Diamond Cutter puts a hog into his pen.

Getting the herd out of the thickets is no easy job—but always accomplished.

would be killed under the feet of the same cattle they just brought to the pens.

Ms. Kathy Grady of Seven Springs, North Carolina, shared with me the work that her Catahoula performs. He herds turkeys from barn to barn. What? You've never heard of such a thing? That's okay, I hadn't either. Ms. Grady said that she places 20,000 turkeys in a brood house and has to move them in about five weeks. She then has to move them again and again until they are about 14 weeks old. She turns out 4,000 head of turkeys from the brood house and lets the Catahoula drive them to the next barn. Like she said, "If you're herding 4,000 turkeys and six turn around, 3,994 are going to follow." The Catahoula, being a natural at bunching a herd, became the answer to her problem. She continues the ordeal until the brood house is empty and readied for the next group to arrive.

The last thing on the list is search-and-rescue and narcotics detecting. I am the handler of a Catahoula who is certified in search-and-rescue work. Ladyhawke is the first Catahoula to receive the Service Champion Award given by National Association of Louisiana Catahoulas (NALC) for her work in search-and-rescue. She has been trained to work in wilderness, water, buildings, evidence location, and cadaver. Together, we work with the Louisiana Search and Rescue Dog Team and the St. Tammany Parish Sheriff's Office. Lady works with other breeds of dogs in the group, and like the other dogs, she is trained to locate people and leave all other animals alone. She has located lost

Note how the dogs on either side taunt the bull while the dog in front holds him in place.

Aden's Angel, Pib and Mariah work a herd. Aden's Luke is learning the ropes.

Mama cow and her baby had to be moved to another pasture—what better way than to use Catahoulas.

Aden's Angel, Bubbles and Mariah hard at work moving cattle.

hunters and missing body parts for law enforcement agencies, as well as several drowning victims. For locating drowned victims she is placed on the bow of a boat. When she has located the scent of the victim she will give a signal, called an alert, which tells me we are within 25 feet of the victim. A diver is then sent in to make the recovery. All of the work is performed at no charge to anyone.

As for narcotic detection, suffice it to say that there are Catahoulas trained to locate various types of narcotics. I cannot go into detail on what training takes place or how it is done, since that would be a violation of law enforcement ethics. The Catahoula will do the same job as any other breed of dog doing this type work. The drive to locate narcotics and please the handler makes the Catahoula a welcome addition to the field of narcotics investigation.

Hunt

What will a Catahoula hunt? Anything. If you want to hunt squirrel, raccoon, rabbit, deer, hogs, bear, mountain lion or anything else, the Catahoula can do it.

The big difference between these dogs and other dogs doing the same hunting is that the Catahoula is silent on the trail. He will not bay or bark until his prey is in sight. There are exceptions, but this is generally the rule. When a Catahoula does bay, the sound will run chills down your spine.

When hunting squirrel or raccoon, the Catahoula does not go for a stroll through the woods looking for prey. He hits the ground running and tracks where the game has been, until the trail gets hot and he trees the prey. That's when the barking starts.

During a show, I had the opportunity to see a treeing contest. A squirrel is placed in a small cage. (The cage is large enough for the squirrel to have room to move around.) The cage is attached to a long rope that has been placed over one of the higher branches of the tree. The cage is then placed on the ground and stays there until a dog is brought up to a starting point about 30 feet away. This allows the dog to see the squirrel and vice versa. When the dog sees the squirrel, he begins barking. When the squirrel sees the dog, he begins moving around in his cage. On a given signal the dog is released, and the cage is raised high enough in the tree so the dog cannot get to the cage or the squirrel. At that time, the counting starts. Three people count the number of barks given by the dog in a one-minute period. The dog with the most barks is the winner. There were 13 dogs entered in this particular show. The winner at that show barked 37 times. The contest for raccoon is held in the same fashion immediately following the squirrel. This is not the place you want to be if you have a headache.

There was a time when a contest called "Coon on a Log" was held for Catahoula owners. A raccoon was placed on a log floating in a pond. The Catahoula would have to swim out to the log and try to get the raccoon off the log. This contest is no longer held since it was decided that the raccoon never won.

When hunting wild hogs, two or three dogs are usually used. The dogs will bay the hog and back him into a corner.

The dogs will work on either side of the hog. One will go in on the hog, and then the other will follow his lead. By doing this, they keep the hog busy watching and fighting back at each dog in turn. The tusks of a hog are very sharp and can cut and even kill a dog. They can certainly inflict a serious wound on a human. If the hog cannot be taken alive, the hunter will kill the hog at that time.

Some hunters will train a Catahoula to be what they call a "catch dog." Three dogs will work together worrying the hog. Two will get on either side of him, and one will get in front. When the signal to catch the hog is given by the hunter, the catch dog, usually in front, will run in and catch an ear or the side of the face. When the catch dog goes in and gets a hold on the hog, one of the other dogs will also run in and grab the other ear or the other side of the hog's face. The third dog will go behind the hog and grab a leg and stretch him out. The three will hold the hog there until the hunters show up and tie the hog. At this point, it's up to the hunters to get in and tie the legs so the hog cannot get up. He is then taken to the pens for cleaning and fattening.

Hunting deer with a Catahoula eliminates looking for your dogs when the hunt is over. The Catahoula is a short-range dog and will usually make it back to camp that same day. If not, leave a blanket on the ground, and he'll be waiting for you in the morning. The question I'm asked most about deer dogs is whether they will track the blood trail of a wounded deer. The best answer to that is: "If you hit him, you'll get him." What makes this such an easy question to answer is that my dog performed a similar task during a test for search-and-rescue work. I was given a scenario of a knife found lying in the road with two drops of blood on it. The dog had to determine if the blood belonged to the *victim* or the *assailant*. The dog made the right decision, and we apprehended the *suspect*. Blood has to run over skin to leave the body. As the blood rolls down the skin, the scent is absorbed into the blood and aids the dog in finding his prey.

As for bear and mountain lion, the dogs will bay them up the same way they do hogs. Usually, two or three dogs are used. You'll have to be fast, though. Catahoulas are impatient. An angry cat or bear can do a lot of damage to your dog while you're making your way to their location.

The first set of puppies I sold for bear hunting was used in Wisconsin. The gentleman came to the kennel and sat with the litter for about an hour and a half. He finally decided on two puppies to take back with him. Six months later he called me and asked if I was expecting any puppies. Thinking something had happened to the other puppies, I asked what had happened to the other dogs. He said: "Nothing, they just put a black bear out of my back yard and I want two more just like them."

Show

Most Catahoulas are shown at sanctioned NALC shows. These shows consist of junior showmanship, obedience, conformation, hog/dog trials, and cow/dog trials.

The cow/dog trials are set up in a field. The hog/dog trials are set up in a fenced pen so that everyone is safe. The handler or rancher, as the case may be, will enter the field and work them as if he were at home. Time limits are set and must be met. The best time wins the event.

The other events like showmanship, obedience and conformation use the same methods as those used by most organizations.

All dogs entered in obedience will have to heel on the left, make turns at the heel, perform a figure eight, stand for examination, sit/stay and down/stay. Sometimes this is hard for Catahoulas. They're used to running. Each dog is graded on his performance, and the one with the highest score is the winner.

In conformation, all dogs are shown in their age brackets, males and females being segregated. All dogs who win in their classes then compete against all the other winners for that day for the best-of-show award. Males and females are still segregated. Each win gains points toward a championship.

Aden's Mariah—a blue Leopard show champion who works cattle.

Abney's Ladyhawke practicing on agility course.

Catahoulas have been shown in some American Kennel Club miscellaneous events and rare-breed shows.

For a more detailed look at what takes place at these events see the chapter on SHOWS.

Guard

In the chapter dealing with the standard, I mention a larger variety of Catahoula. These larger dogs are the ones that are mostly used for guarding by private industry because they are more intimidating. The larger type appears to have a shorter life span and tends to take longer

Blair's Sampson, owned by Don Abney, stands guard in the kennel.

to mature. These dogs do not fit the standard of the Catahoula and therefore are not a favorable type for the purpose of showing.

The type that falls into the standard will work equally well and will mature faster than the larger ones.

As for sounding an alarm, the Catahoula will do that anytime a stranger comes near. This is a natural response and doesn't need to be taught.

Samantha Treder with Sanglier's Beausoleil. Junior Showmanship builds character and children enjoy being able to participate in a show with a pet.

Pet

A Catahoula makes a great pet. As I stated earlier, he is a natural protector of his family. Children that are raised around a Catahoula know that their dog will protect them no matter what the situation, yet the dog will play and be a friend to all around him. The one thing I tell everyone is to make arrangements for obedience training when the dog is six months old. Obedience does not mean that you are going to show your dog. It means that your dog will learn a few basic commands to keep him out of trouble and make you the boss. Obedience training does not cost a lot of money. Besides, you just spent money buying a dog, so why not protect that investment with obedience classes?

Pets can be a real pain in the neck for children playing. The dog does not want the children to make noise. Each noise makes the dog check on them. Squealing children can really aggravate a Catahoula and start him barking. He cannot determine why the children are crying out. Placing them away from the children isn't much better. Now he worries that he can't take care of them. Believe me, you have to own a Catahoula to understand.

I must say that the Catahoula, as amazing as he can be, is not for everyone. The Catahoula must have room to run. If this dog is not allowed to run, he will destroy everything around him. A Catahoula cannot be penned up and forgotten. He will not let you forget.

If you decide to make a house dog of him, you must realize that your furniture is at stake. These dogs need exercise. Playing ball, obedience exercises and a good run are perfect. Crate training is a must. Remember, this dog is very wary of strangers. If someone comes to your house while the dog is loose inside, it will drive him crazy.

Chapter 5

STANDARD

In the beginning, the Catahoula standard was something like this: "If it works like a Catahoula, looks like a Catahoula, acts like a Catahoula, then it must be a Catahoula."

I know that sounds too simple, but that's the way it was.

The Catahoula was a large wolf-like dog standing approximately 28 inches in height at the withers and weighing up to 100 pounds. The dog is described as having a very squared head, large massive chest, and large bones. There is nothing wrong with this type dog, especially if you are looking for a dog to do guard work. There are still some breeders around that breed for this size dog. However, it has been studied and found that a medium to medium-large Catahoula can do herding work for a longer time and will live longer than his larger counterpart.

Through the years, the Catahoula has undergone some transitions. Some have crossed the Catahoula with other breeds, trying to improve on the animal, but, through it all, they eventually returned to the standard Catahoula.

In 1984, the breeding members of the NALC developed a standard to gauge the Catahoula. The following is the standard that is used today.

General Impression

The Louisiana Catahoula is a medium to medium-large dog; well-muscled, yet trim, powerful, but denoting agility and great endurance.

Head:

The head should be powerfully built with a broad top skull and well-developed cheeks. The muzzle should be strong and deep and approximately equal in length to the top skull as measured from the stop to the occiput bone. The muzzle should be broad at the base and taper toward the nose when viewed from the front.

The stop should be moderate in length and well defined.

Bite:

The bite should be a strong scissor bite, with a level bite being acceptable.

> Serious Faults: Overshot or undershot bites

Ears:

The ears should be short to medium in length with the top of the ear being set level or slightly below the top of the head. Properly hung ears, with the inner edge of the ear lying close to the cheek are preferred. "Laid back" ears are acceptable.

> Faults: Fly-a-way, houndish, or cropped ears are to be penalized.

Eyes:

Glass eyes are preferred, although the eyes may be of any color or combination of colors. The eyes do not have to be the same color.

> Faults: Malformed or acentric pupils

Fore Assembly:

The length of the foreleg should be 50 to 60 percent of the total height of the dog as measured from the ground to the top of the withers. The neck should be muscular and of good length. The shoulders should be well laid back with an upper arm bone of ample length. The forelegs should be set moderately far apart and the front feet should toe neither in nor out.

Chest, Body and Back:

The chest should be deep reaching below the elbow. The chest should be fairly broad with well-sprung ribs. The back should be strong

Above: Two Diamond's Dakota, owned by Jeff and Jeanne Treder.
Below: Closeup of Two Diamond's Dakota's head. Note the "glass eyes."

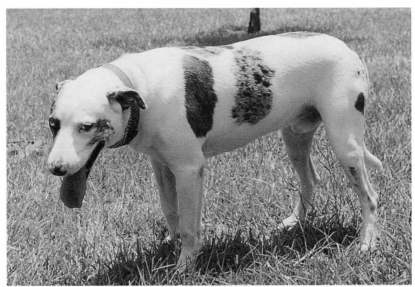

Abney's Patches—a typical patch coloration.

Abney's Tabasco—an 18-month-old black Leopard with red trim.

and well muscled, level and of medium length. The underline should have tuck-up in the loin area to a moderate degree.

Rear Assembly:

The croup should be medium to long in length and slightly sloping with the tail having a medium to high set. The stifles should be angular and the hocks should be set low to the ground. The hocks should turn neither in nor out when viewed from the rear.

Faults: Bobtail

Feet:

The feet should be strong and moderate in length. Good webbing between the toes should be evident. Dew claws may be present or removed but if present should be uniform.

Faults: Cat-footed (up on tip-toes); Coon-footed (standing on heels)

Coat Length:

The coat should be short to medium in length.

Disqualifications: Long and/or fuzzy coats

Coat Color:

Leopards are to be preferred and may come in blue, gray, black, liver, red, white and patched. Trim may be black, white, tan, red or buff. Solid colors acceptable are black, brindle, red, chocolate and yellow.

Size:

Females should measure 20-24 inches at the top of the withers. Males should measure 22-26 inches at the top of the withers.

In both sexes, the medium of the extremes is to be preferred.

Faults: Animals either undersized or oversized with the severity of the penalty being based upon the degree of non-conformity.

This written description depicts the ideal Louisiana Catahoula. Any deviation from the described ideal will be judged accordingly and in proportion to the deviation:

STRUCTURAL FAULTS WILL BE JUDGED MORE HARSHLY THAN COSMETIC FAULTS.

These are the standards as written by NALC. The exception to cosmetic faults refers to a dog that works and is also shown. Working dogs will pick up injuries and scars, and these faults will not be judged against the dog.

The term cosmetic does not mean that the organization, or any of the breeders, condones any surgery to make the dog that is to be shown look better than its natural state.

Abney's Blue Bear—a blue Leopard with classic trim.

Chapter 6

SHOW

In the chapter headed Uses, I gave a brief description of what takes place at a dog show. I find that most people stay away from dog shows because they do not know what is expected of them or their dogs; however, there are five events that can be fun, informative and rewarding. These events are conformation, obedience, showmanship, cow/dog trials, and hog/dog trials. It is your choice to participate in any one or all of them.

Conformation compares your dog to the standard as set by NALC as well as all the other dogs being shown. If you are a breeder, this helps you determine if you are doing the right thing with your breeding program. If you are a pet owner you will learn how well your dog conforms to the standard. You may find that you have a dog that is worthy of breeding. Spayed and neutered pets may not be shown in conformation events.

Obedience trials are fun and rewarding. It is fun to see how well your dog will perform in competition with other dogs doing the same routine. The rewards are that you have a dog who knows what to do and when to do it. The level of obedience is really up to you. You may want to go on to a higher level of obedience or just stay at your present level. Spayed and neutered pets are allowed to participate in these events.

Showmanship events will help you become a better handler. You will learn techniques that will help your dog become a better performer, and you will learn the true meaning of sportsmanship. Generally, this event is for younger handlers, ages 8 through 18, but there are things adults can learn by watching these events.

Cow/dog trials are set up in a fenced field with a holding pen set up at one end. The object here is for the rancher, generally on horseback, along with his dog(s), up to three, to work five cows in the ring and then pen them. This must be accomplished in a certain time frame.

Hog/dog trials are set up in a fenced area called the pen. The handler and his dog enter the pen and work the hog. The dog must bay up the hog and hold him at bay for a prescribed time.

Your dog must be up to date on all of his shots before being shown in any event. This requirement is an attempt to prevent the spread of diseases.

I hope the following information will help those reluctant owners begin attending shows and exhibiting their dogs.

Conformation Trials:

To show a dog in a conformation event, your dog will need a minimum amount of obedience training. Don't get discouraged by the words obedience training. This is not difficult and can be accomplished by working with your dog a few minutes a day. These few minutes are what scares most people. All that is needed is about 15 minutes a day for about two weeks. That's all it takes, however you must establish a rapport with your dog so he will put forth his best effort to please you.

When watching dog shows, you can hear comments like "look how proudly that dog walks." His head is held high; he is moving in a positive manner with a fluid motion. This is the rapport you are looking for in your dog. He will walk proud if he knows he is pleasing you.

Remember when working with your dog, there must also be some play time as well. After a good workout, play a game of fetch for another few minutes, or take a walk, or do whatever your dog likes to do. Knowing that he can play when the work is done will make him work even harder. Training must be fun. If it is a yelling match between you

Blue Sky's Cricket, owned and shown by Janette Blair.

and a dog that doesn't comprehend your language, you'll be wasting your time and confusing your dog. There are many books that help teach obedience training, but none compare to attending an obedience class.

Your dog will have to heel at your left side. He must be able to walk at a normal walking speed and a trot. He must be able to stand for examination. This means that the dog must allow the judge to touch him.

Here is how a conformation show usually works. All males and females are separated and then placed into different groups. The groups are set up according to the age of the dog. Males are shown together and females are shown together. In this manner, you will be showing your dog against dogs of the same sex and general age as yours. For example: 3-6 month males, 3-6 month females, 6-9 month males, 6-9 month females, etc.

Before the show starts you will be given a number to wear on your sleeve. This identifies you as the handler for the dog that is being shown for that particular event. You will be placed in a staging area along with all the dogs in that class. This gives the handlers and dogs a place to assemble before being called to the ring. This is the time for getting that upbeat attitude—before entering the ring. Some handlers will wait until they enter the ring to begin pumping up their dogs. I like to get him attentive before he enters the ring. This way, when you enter the ring your dog is paying attention to you and what he is supposed to be doing. This will help get the attention of the judge. You want the judge's attention.

Upon entering, you will be told to circle the ring. All the dogs in the class will circle the ring two or three times. As you are circling, the judge will be checking the gait of all the dogs in the ring.

The judge will stop the parade and tell you to stack your dog. This is a stand for examination posture. The dog is stood erect in his best pose. The judge will walk up to the dog from the side. He will look at the dog and move to the front and then to the back. Next, he will place his hands on the dog's head and check his eyes and teeth. When the judge checks your dog's eyes, he is looking at the formation of the pupils, not the color. When he checks the teeth, he is looking for the type of bite the dog possesses. He will pass his hands over the front quarters of the dog, then feel the top line, backbone and shoulders for any flaws. Here he is checking for bone structure, bone length and formation. Next, he will examine the hind quarters, and, if this is a male class, he will check the testicles to insure both have descended.

When he is finished, he will ask you to take your dog down and back. He will generally point in the direction he wants you to go. You will take your dog and trot him out about 50 feet, turn around, and bring the dog back to the judge. He will then thank you and proceed with the next dog. You must stack your dog again and wait until the judge has checked all the dogs. The reason for restacking is to give the judge a chance to take a second look at your dog if he is comparing two dogs that are close in contention. The judge may ask everyone to parade the dogs around the ring again. He will then make his decision, and the awards for that class will be handed out.

There are four places that can be won. Points are awarded for each place in the class up to fourth place. When you have won the first-place ribbon, you will be asked to return to the final show ring at the end of all other shows for that day. This is called the winners ring. Now your dog will be competing against all the winners of the same sex for that day. The winner of this competition is the Best of Show (male and female) winner. There is a runner-up as well. Additional points are awarded to the Best of Show and Reserve Best of Show winners. You

Setting up for the judge—this is not always as easy as it appears.

Show Time! Note the different colors.

will have to accrue a required number of points awarded by three different judges to gain the title of Champion.

Please keep in mind that this is what takes place at a sanctioned show. Other organizations may differ in the structure of the show and placement, but all are very similar.

Obedience Trials:

At obedience trials, all work will be performed in the ring individually with the exception of the long sit, and the long down, which is done as a group. Level 1 will be performed with the dog on lead. Level 2 will be performed with the dog off lead.

Again, I recommend that your dog be taken to an experienced obedience instructor for training. This does not mean that you cannot teach your dog the fundamentals. It only gives you the advantage of an instructor to correct any problems the dog or you may have with training. An experienced instructor will be able to break bad habits you or your dog may be forming. Even with the help of an instructor you will be the one training the dog.

Well, it's show time and here is what you will be doing. You will enter the ring and stand where the judge tells you. Your dog should be sitting at your left. The judge will instruct you through all phases of the trial. If at any time you should have a problem understanding a command, stop and raise your hand. The judge will explain it to you.

First, you will be instructed to heel your dog. You will walk in a straight line. The judge will call out for left turn, right turn, about turn, fast, slow, normal and halt. These commands will not necessarily be in the order written.

Next, you will heel your dog through a figure eight. There may be two objects in the ring, or there may be two people. You will have to perform the figure eight around them.

The next thing is to stand for examination. You will place your dog in a standing position and step away from him. The judge will examine the dog just as a conformation judge would. Your dog must stay and allow the judge to touch him. When the judge has completed the exam he will tell you to return to your dog. The dog must not move until you are in the heel position and the judge releases you.

You will then be told to put you dog in a sit-stay and leave the dog. This is the recall. The dog must come to you on the first call and sit in

Aubrey Aden holding the Best in Show female Aden's Pib's Angel and Louis Smith with the Reserve Best of Show female Blue Sky's Poppy. That's what shows are all about.

Aden's Luke, a light-red Leopard. This dog became a champion show dog in 14 months.

Abney's Ladyhawke. NALC's first Service Award Champion in Search & Rescue. Holder of the Excellence in Training Award prersented by Sigma Chemical Corporation.

Brothers Balentine's Mr. Buckets, owned and shown by Clyde Keating, and Balentine's Shadow, owned and shown by Don Abney.

front of you without the benefit of another command or signal. The judge will then tell you to finish your dog. You will give whatever command you have chosen to have your dog return to the heel position. The judge will then give the command to release the dog.

After each dog has had a chance to complete this phase, the judge will call all dogs entered in obedience to the ring. It is at this time that the long sit and the long down will be performed. Your dog will have to sit unattended with all the other dogs for one to three minutes. Then he will have to stay in the long down for three to five minutes. The time frames given vary with each organization.

When all the testing is completed, the judge will tell you the exercise is completed. The judge will then tally up all the scores and award the ribbons for first through fourth places.

Level 2 is performed in a similar manner, except you will not be allowed to use your lead. There will also be some jumps added to the event. Points are awarded just as with conformation. An explanation of these events and point placement will be found in the NALC handbook.

Showmanship Trials:

In this event you will be judged how well you work with your dog. You are the one being judged. All entrants will be asked to perform the same tasks that are performed in the conformation show ring. The handlers are separated into groups by age and sex. The handlers will work their dogs, and the judge will be watching their every move. The judge will award the ribbons for first through forth places.

This is fun and can really help you learn what to do with a dog who is difficult to show. It will make a better sport of you if you have the knowledge of what it takes to show a dog.

Cow/Dog Trials:

In cow/dog trials you may use up to three dogs. All work by the handler will be done from horseback. There will be two field judges, also on horseback, observing and keeping time. You will have 25 minutes to move a minimum of three head of cattle across a field and into a pen. You will then move them out of the pen and into a corral.

There are seven categories in which you are judged in an attempt to obtain the highest score:

Control of Cattle (dog)
The dogs are being judged how well they group up the cattle and keep them moving across the field.

Team Work (dog)
The judges determine how well the dogs work together. An example of this is, if a dog leaves to pick up a stray, the others will take up the slack until he returns. Scoring for this depends upon the number of dogs being used. If three dogs are being used, each dog will wear a piece of flagging tape on his collar: red, white or blue. If two dogs are used, only red and white tape will be used. If only one dog is used, he will wear red tape on his collar. Each working dog will then carry a predetermined number of points he may earn.

Bay Up
A contestant may call a bay up at any time during his run. The term bay up is used when the dogs have grouped the cattle together and held them in that position, without wandering, for two minutes.

Stock
Since the cattle are changed with each run, there is no way to tell how the herd will respond. The judges will determine the difficulty of the herd. The harder it is to work the cattle, the higher the points.

Cowboying
The contestant is given points at the start of his run and points are deducted each time he has to assist his dogs. Giving commands and directions are not discounted, but physical assistance is.

Middle Pen
For each cow that is penned you will receive points. The dogs must assist in the penning of the cattle. Once this is done, if it is done, the cattle must be moved out and down to the corral.

End Pen

This is the corralling. Each contestant must pen all the cattle and close the gate at the end of his run. When this is completed, the contestant will be given 10 minutes to catch and secure his dogs. If the dogs are not secured within 10 minutes, the run will be disqualified. The handler, better known as the contestant, may whistle, yell or use a whip to get the attention of his dogs. The whip is used only to make a noise and is not used on the dogs or the cattle. An additional handler may be used to release the dogs at the start of a run, but he must leave the field immediately after the dogs are released. The same handler may be used in retrieving the dogs at the end of their run.

Hog/Dog Trials:

In this event, only the handler in the ring may give commands to the dog. An assistant may be used to release and retrieve the dog at the beginning and end of the run. The assistant must leave the ring immediately after the dog is released or retrieved. Each entrant will have three minutes to catch and secure the dog after his set is completed. Failure to secure the dog will result in disqualification.

Before a run begins, the entrant must give the name and sex of the dog to the timekeeper.

The entrant must inform the timekeeper if he desires a different hog from the one that is presently in the ring. If another hog is chosen, the entrant must take the next hog out of the chute.

If the entrant wants a warm-up for his dog, he must notify the timekeeper. He will then be given a 30-second warm up. The time begins when the dog is released.

The hog will be released from a chute, pen or trailer. The time begins when the dog is released or after the 30-second warm-up. Remember, the warm-up must be requested before the start of the run.

The Judge's Word is Final

There may be one or more judges, depending on the hog/dog trial host. The judge has the right to determine if a "too-rough" dog should be removed from the ring. If the dog is too rough during the three-minute removal time, he may be disqualified.

The judge may decide whether or not to replace a hog. If another hog should escape into the ring while a dog is working, the handler will take instructions from the judge only.

If a dog should catch the hog, it will be given a warning on the first two catches. If the dog catches for a third time, it will be disqualified. If any catch is for longer than 15 seconds, the dog will be disqualified.

Scoring

First event: In a one-dog one-hog event, only one handler may be in the ring and on foot. There will be 20 entries. All scores will be tallied and awards given for first through fourth places.

Second event: Here two dogs may be used. There will be four or more hogs in the ring in this event. There can be no more than two handlers in the ring with the dogs. At the end of the runs, all scores will be tallied and awards for first through fourth places will be awarded.

High Point Dog. All points will be tallied, and the Catahoula with the highest score will be named HIGH POINT DOG. Second highest points will be named RESERVE HIGH POINT DOG.

Blair's Gator Jr., shown by Janette Blair. He is sire to World Hog Champion Blair's Bubba.

In case of a tie, the decision will be made by 1) control/bay up, 2) distance or 3) coin flip.

Points are gained in the following areas: Control/Bay Up, Interest, Distance (the shorter the better), Stock (ease of handling) and Participation.

In two-dog events, each dog will be judged individually.

Now that you understand what is expected of you and your dogs at any of the events, you should be making plans to participate in the next show. If you feel that you are not ready for participation, come out and join us by being a spectator. Some owners have come out just to watch a show. Then, when the show was over, they were asking when and where the next show would be held, and how could they enter.

There are other champion degrees that your dog may acquire in addition to those stated above. A copy of the NALC handbook may be obtained by writing to: NALC, POB 1041, Denham Springs, LA., 70727. This handbook will provide the rules and point system currently in place and what must be accomplished to obtain champion status.

When I told you the shows could be fun, it was the truth. Watching a group of Catahoula owners helping each other, exchanging ideas, and telling stories just to improve the breed speaks highly of these dedicated people.

Hope to see you at the next show!

*Two Diamond's Dakota and Samantha
Treder. Smiling faces all around for this
first-place winner.*

Chapter 7

PURCHASING

If you have decided that a Catahoula is the dog for you, there are a few things you should do before acquiring one.

First, try to locate a few certified breeders. The term *certified* in this case means that the breeder is registered with the NALC. These breeders have agreed to breed only registered Catahoulas in compliance with the standard and regulations set forth by that organization.

Not all breeders are certified breeders but may own registered dogs. So, the next question is whether this was a planned breeding or an accidental one. If it was accidental, there could be some resultant genetic problems. A check of genealogy and genetic backgrounds of the mating pair should be done to insure that the pups will be healthy and show no genetic defects.

Planned breeding requires a background check of the bloodlines to insure that a genetic problem does not occur. These are the steps a responsible breeder would take before breeding his dogs.

Next, you might ask how many dogs are owned and for what purpose they are used. This will give you a general idea as to what you will be purchasing. For example, if you are looking for a dog for show, and

Abney's Cash Money, owned by Damian Weyland of New York, peeking out the window.

the breeder uses his dogs for working cows, this may not be the dog you would want to see. This does not mean that a working dog cannot be a show dog. It only informs you that the breeder is looking for one aspect of the breed and not necessarily the quality you would want for show. Most owners of working dogs are not interested in the looks of the dog. They want only a dog that will work.

Now that you have those answers, go see the kennel. The old saying, "a picture is worth a thousand words," will ring true when you view the kennel.

Keep in mind that you are not looking at whether the kennel is dirt, gravel or concrete. You are looking for cleanliness. This will be your first indication that the breeder cares about his animals. Observe the amount of feces in the pens. It is always a possibility that a dog will leave some between cleanings, but there should not be large amounts in the pens. Pay attention to the odors. Puppies that are in the same pen will have an odor about them because of the continuous playing that takes place; however, this is the only odor that should be present. Watch for flies. There may be a few flies in the area, which is normal at various times of the year, but you should not be irritated by flies while observing the dogs. This statement about flies also depends upon whether the kennel is part of a barn-type system. If other animals such as cattle or goats are in the same vicinity as the dogs, it is almost impossible to eliminate the pests.

Look at the dogs closely. Do not pay attention to what the whelping female looks like. She is keeping up a food supply for herself and the pups and is in the stage of getting her system back in order. Also, do not look at the puppies first. All puppies are cute. I haven't found anyone who would say they saw an ugly puppy in any litter.

You want to see if the other dogs in the kennel are healthy looking or if they look as if they are on death's front door. If a breeder cares about his dogs, it will show in the kennel.

Well, what do you know, you've found the right puppy. Wait! How much of a white coat does the pup have? One of the genetic defects of a Catahoula is that 80 percent of white-faced puppies with glass eyes will be deaf, blind or sterile. Be sure you test the dog before going any further. Ask the breeder if there any guarantees. If so, what are they? Is the guarantee in writing? Most breeders will guarantee their pups to be free of genetic defects and parasites at the time of purchase. Some breeders will ask you to visit your veterinarian within 10 to 15 days after your purchase or your guarantee is void. This is not an unreasonable request. The reason behind this is to insure that the purchaser takes the pup to a veterinarian. Since your pup should have been wormed and had his first puppy shot, it would be time for the next shot at about 15 days. Besides, you want to insure you have made a good purchase and that your puppy is healthy.

Check the documents that are required to register your new acquisition. You should be presented with a blue sheet of paper, commonly called puppy papers, that will contain information concerning the lineage of your pup.

The breeder will fill out the necessary portions of the form such as sex, eye color and coat color, and he will sign the form. Ask the breeder for the puppy identification number. This number is on the stub that the breeder keeps for his records. For example, the litter number of this litter may be 3424. The puppy's identification number will be 3424-(#). The information on the stub corresponds to the information on your sheet. If anything should happen to your puppy papers, you will be able to call your breeder and have him track your papers or assist you in getting your puppy registered.

You will be responsible for filling in the name of your pet, your name and address, and mailing the papers to receive your Registration Certificate.

You will notice that the space for the name of your pup already shows a name. This is the kennel name and shows no ownership whatsoever. This is only for kennel identification purposes.

If you are purchasing an older dog that has already been registered, you should be presented with the Registration Certificate. This assures that the dog has been registered. On the back of the Registration is a place for the owner to sign and date the sale. You will have to fill out the required information and mail it along with the prescribed amount to have the dog registered in your name. You will be issued a new Registration Certificate showing your ownership. You should ask the owner about the dog's medical history and any records he may have. Ask the name of the veterinarian that cared for the dog. You will want to ask this veterinarian about the dog, as well as have your own veterinarian check him over. As before, ask if there are any guarantees. Don't be

Blair's Bubba—World Champion Hog Dog.

shy. It's your money, and, if it were a sewing machine or chain saw, you'd ask the salesman about the guarantee.

The decision to buy a dog does not have to hinge on the guarantee. It only tells you that the breeder or owner believes that what he is doing is the right thing and is willing to meet you half way if there is a problem. Usually, there are none.

I usually give the buyer the option of the following:

> 1. If there is a genetic problem, bring the puppy back with the vet's certificate; I will refund your money.
>
> 2. Bring the puppy back, and I will replace it with another from my kennel or help you find one from another kennel.
>
> 3. If there is a birth problem that can be corrected and you want to keep the pup, I will split the vet bill with you 50/50.

A good breeder wants to know if there are any problems, so they can be corrected in future breeding. The problem could stem from somewhere in the background, and the breeder would want to make a more intense study before breeding these dogs again.

If you cannot find a breeder in your immediate area, or, if you do not find the exact puppy you want, you will have to go outside your area.

If you are dealing with a breeder over long distances the questions are the same. Although you cannot observe the kennel, you can get pictures. You will want a breeder who is familiar with shipping animals and the steps that need to be taken to get your pup to you safely.

Keep in mind that the price of the pup is not the only price consideration. It is only the start. There are shipping charges, shipping crate, veterinarian health certificate not more than 10 days old, and an acclamation certificate to be dealt with. A major inconvenience in some instances is the airlines' rule of not shipping a puppy if the temperatures are below 45 degrees or above 85 degrees. It is an excellent rule, however, since it is for the protection of the pup. It also means that, if the pup has to change flights and the temperature is not in those ranges at the point of change, your pup may be held up until he can be shipped. This will generally occur if you are not in the vicinity of a major airport and a commuter flight has to be used to reach the final destination.

I had this problem once, and the pup was held by the airlines until the weather permitted shipping it the next day. I am pleased to report that the airlines put the puppy in a veterinarian's office, where he was cleaned, fed and provided with a place to sleep for the night. The crate was cleaned and ready for shipping the next day. All this was done at no charge to either end.

The airlines have really improved the way they handle the shipping of animals. The cargo areas of passenger planes are now climate controlled so the animals do not have any difficulty with the temperatures of higher altitudes. This does not include commuter flights, which may not be climate controlled.

One of the things I offer a customer is to buy back the shipping crate. I know the puppy is going to outgrow it, so I give the customer the opportunity to ship the crate back to me for a refund of its cost. Crates vary in cost according to size. I can reuse the crate, and it helps defray some of the customer's expense of shipping the puppy.

"May I come out now?" Blair's Gumbo, owned by Janette Blair, asks.

Chapter 8

CARE AND MAINTENANCE

The first question I am asked after the purchase of a puppy or an adult dog is: "What kind of food are you feeding them?" I take them to the storeroom, show them the bags of food with the labels intact, and explain what they mean. I know they only wanted to know the name of the food, but I feel that, if they want to know the name of the food, they should know why I chose it.

The Association of American Feed Control Officials and the Food and Drug Administration regulate the nutritional requirements of the dog-food industry. It is required that the first ingredient on the ingredients' label be the primary ingredient in volume. The second ingredient should be the secondary ingredient, and so on. When it comes down to the vitamins and minerals in the food, most are the same. Note, I said most. This is because these ingredients are purchased as pre-measured items by the food producers. Lastly, there are the preservatives. You must make your own decision as to what you think are good preservatives.

I tell my customers that any dry dog food that has beef, chicken or fish as the first ingredient on the label is a good food for your dog. Also, the byproducts of these ingredients are good but not as good as the real thing.

Also important are the protein and fat percentages. I like to feed an active dog a 22-26 percent protein food containing about 15-20 percent fat. This is good for your active adult dog as well as your puppy. Puppies require a food with high protein and fat contents, because they are growing and are more active than most adult dogs. If you check the labels on food classified as puppy food, you will see that the fat content is usually between 15 and 20 percent.

Do not feed large amounts of whole milk to newly acquired puppies. This will lead to soft stools and may cause diarrhea. Should this occur, give one-half of normal diet as cooked white rice. Also, a puppy's stomach should not look like a balloon when he is finished eating.

Puppies should be fed two or three times a day until they are between six and eight months old. Then you may start feeding them once a day, but give them the total amount of food that you were feeding them. It is important to watch your puppy when you start feeding once a day. The puppy should finish eating his food within 15 minutes. If there is food left over, pick it up. If he looks as if he is looking for more to eat, give it to him. Healthy puppies make healthy dogs.

Older dogs beyond the age of eight do not require high amounts of protein because they are not as active. You can cut your cost by feeding a food with a lesser amount of protein and fat content, or you may reduce the amount of food you are feeding them and not change the food at all.

Be careful when changing your foods. Sudden changes in food types or intake can cause diarrhea. A change in food brands or contents should be done over a five-day period. Increase the new food gradually, even if it's the same brand.

What about table scraps? NO. NO. NO. Giving table scraps to your dog may be a convenient way for you to dispose of your food waste, but your dog is not a garbage disposal. There are nutrients in dry dog foods that your dog needs. The dry foods of today have everything your dog needs. Table scraps do not have these necessary ingredients. Think about this the next time you want to give your dogs your leftovers.

Canned dog foods are about 70 percent water. That is a strong statement for me to make, or so I am told. Some manufacturers will put on their labels that only the amount of water necessary for cooking is used. Okay, so why does the label show water as the first ingredient? We have already explained it. The rules for wet foods are the same as for dry, with the first ingredient as the primary ingredient.

Since we are talking about water, the one thing that most owners do not understand is water. A dog could go hungry for a day or two, but he should never go thirsty. Clean, fresh water should always be available to your dog. They can withstand hunger, but they cannot withstand thirst. Water helps their digestive system as well as quenches their thirst and keeps them cool. Check twice daily to see that your dog has a good supply of water readily available to him.

Where to Keep Your Dog

There are yards, homes, kennels, runs and that spot under the oak tree. You should understand that problems may occur with any of these locations. If you keep your dog in your home, he will have to be trained to relieve himself outdoors. This is your problem and not the dog's. There is the problem of fleas getting in the house. You will have to wash and dip your dog regularly. And don't forget to clip those nails.

Keeping him in a yard is good. The only problem you've eliminated is your dog messing up your house and smelling bad. You still have to wash and dip the dog and treat the yard. You still have to clip those nails, and now he is digging up the yard so that it looks like a battlefield. Some fun, huh?

Okay, it's not over yet. Let's put him on a concrete run. Now you don't have to clip those nails. Now he has sores on the elbows and tops of his feet because the concrete causes calluses. As he gets older, the hard surface affects his joints, making it hard for him to get around. It is easier to clean, but the ground around the run is always wet and messy.

Looks like you have figured out that a dog is a lot of work, even if you don't want to admit it. How much trouble can one dog be? Plenty, if he is not cared for properly. A dog needs the company of his master. He needs someone to play with him and show him attention. He needs to belong to the family or have a bond with someone in the family. Dogs suffer severely from boredom. These are usually the dogs that are referred to as "a pain in the neck."

Dogs need obedience training. You should register your dog in an obedience class when he is about six months old. Learn how to handle your dog. Make him understand who is the boss and what he can or cannot do. A dog who knows the rules is a happier dog than one that does not—even the hard rules. Why? Because dogs love to please their masters. A dog that knows and obeys the rules will not be scolded. This makes the dog happy. A dog that does not know the rules never knows when he is going to be scolded or praised.

Finally, I want to mention that spot under the oak tree. It is not fair to the dog to get tied or chained to a tree. He never gets to investigate the odd things that crop up around the yard. He gets scolded, because he is always barking to get off the chain. Pups that spend the first year of their life on chains become neurotic, and often never adjust to a normal dog's life. Dogs are pack animals and need a pack, even if you are the pack leader. Isolation is more punishment to them than if you had beaten them with a broomstick. No, I don't condone beating your dog, nor do I agree with tying him to a tree. Just don't do it!

Any dog that is kept outdoors should have a good shelter of his own to keep him from the elements. This is a doghouse. The doghouse may be constructed of many different materials. You decide which you prefer. The door of the doghouse should face southward away from the prevailing north winds. I find a house with the door off center is best. It allows the dog room inside to escape the cold wind in the winter. A door in the center of the house allows the cold wind to enter and circulate all over the inside. The dog cannot escape the wind. Hay or pine straw are excellent floor covers in winter and will help keep him warm. What about summer? He will come out of his house and find a shady spot. If there are no shady spots available in his yard then provide an overhang on the front of his house. He has no need to stay in the house unless it rains. Again, it provides an escape from the elements.

Your dog should be washed and brushed on a regular basis. A Catahoula's coat is short and easily kept clean. Washing should not occur more than every two weeks. Brushing daily, though not necessary, will help keep him clean.

Here's a tip on washing your dog: Brush him before his bath. This will remove some of the loose dirt and hair. There's no use in washing loose hair. I have found that placing a dog in a tub of water makes him nervous and he will fight the bath. If you place him in a dry tub and use a sprayer, it is much easier and the dog is more comfortable about the bath. This makes it easier on you to clean him. Also if you use liquid soap, as I do, it's much easier to place the soap on the dog first then wet the dog with water and wash him. Using a sprayer will ensure that you are rinsing your dog with clean water instead of using the water that accumulates in the tub. Spraying will remove all the soap. If soap is allowed to remain on the dog, it will dry out his skin.

I have listed some of the more frequently encountered problems and what can be done to remedy them. This may seem too simplified to the trained professional, but my intention is to educate and not prescribe. It should also be understood that, any time you have a problem and you're not absolutely sure of the cause or the cure, seek the advice of a veterinarian.

Internal Parasites

There are five types of worms that are most important. They are: roundworm, hookworm, tapeworm, whipworm, and heartworm. Each has its own distinctive characteristics and symptoms. All can be treated, but all can cause death if not corrected. The best treatment is prevention.

D.C.'s Jumping Jack Flash, owned by Jeff and Jeanne Treder. It's easy to see that he has no health problems.

Roundworm

Roundworms are generally present in newborn puppies. Puppies are born with them and must be treated. The whelping bitch should be treated at the same time you treat her puppies. The worm comes from the dormant larvae in the muscles of the bitch. When she becomes pregnant, the larvae become active and move into the fetus. When the puppies are born, the larvae are already in them. Within one week of birth, the larvae will travel to the intestines and mature. Infestation in dogs that are over the age of six weeks is accomplished a little differently. The dog will swallow the egg, which will develop and migrate to the lungs and be coughed up. The larvae are then swallowed, and the worm will develop in the small intestines.

Signs: Infected pups will appear pot-bellied. Only the stomach will be fat, while the rest of the puppy will look poor. The coat will be dull. Diarrhea with excessive mucous will be evident. Dead adult worms may be seen in the stool. They look like pieces of string or spaghetti. The bitch should be wormed, since she has been licking and cleaning the newborn puppies. This will put the worm's life cycle back in motion. The eggs can be detected by use of a fecal exam under a microscope.

Treatment: *Pyrantel* or *Febantel* are two of the better remedies. Treatment of the puppies should begin between two and three weeks of age. It will require giving the puppies an oral liquid based on their body weight. A subsequent treatment is recommended approximately 10 days after the first. The same treatment is recommended for the whelping female.

Hookworm

An infected dog will pass hookworm eggs in his feces between 15 and 20 days after being infected. The eggs will hatch in a warm, moist soil in 24 to 72 hours. Infection occurs by ingestion. Nursing puppies will ingest the larvae while feeding. Infection in adults as well as puppies can occur by larval invasion of the skin. The larvae migrate through the blood to the lungs, where they can be coughed up and swallowed. They will then attach themselves to the lining of the intestines by means of a hooked mouth and begin sucking blood.

Signs: Anemia can be detected by examining the color of the dog's gums. The gums should be pink, and, when pressed with your finger, should turn white. The color should restore within about two seconds. The gums of an anemic animal will appear white and no noticeable change will be detected when pressed. Pups are usually thin and most will have diarrhea with or without the presence of blood.

Another way to detect the presence of hookworm is to have a fecal exam. The worm eggs may be seen under a microscope.

Treatment: Hookworm is treated the same as roundworm with *Pyrantel* or *Febantel* administered orally according to body weight. There are several other good worm medications. Consult your veterinarian.

Tapeworm

Most infections of tapeworm are acquired by means of flea bites. The larvae travel through the saliva of the flea to the dog. The larvae then migrate to the intestines, where they mature. The tapeworm has a voracious appetite. However, it does not suck blood.

Signs: The tapeworm may be seen in the feces of infected animals. It will look like a grain of rice or cucumber seed. As it moves, it will elongate. Hence the name tapeworm. The dog will have an enormous appetite and his coat will be dull and shaggy. The dog may also suffer from a mild case of diarrhea.

Treatment: *Praziquantel* is administered according to body weight. Your veterinarian will have this in a tablet or injectable form. To prevent tapeworms, fleas need to be eradicated. Simply keeping the flea population down will help the war against this pest.

Whipworm

Whipworms are acquired through ingestion. The eggs are passed in the feces and hatch in two to four weeks in a warm, moist environment. The larvae travel to the small intestines where they feed until maturity. This takes about 11 weeks. The larvae may remain here for up to 16 months. This worm is commonly found in confined dogs, such as those chained or held in small dog yards on dirt.

Signs: Weight loss, diarrhea and anemia. Fresh blood may be seen in the feces.

Treatment: The successful treatment of adult worms may be accomplished with *Fenbendazole*. It will require three consecutive days of treatment. The eggs of the whipworm may remain viable for up to five years in warm, moist areas, including the cracks in concrete. The best preventive medicine for this worm is hygiene. Keep the dog's yard and sleeping quarters clean and dry.

Heartworm

When a mosquito bites a dog that is positive for heartworm, it ingests the microfilaria that are present in the blood. This remains in the mosquito for approximately two weeks. The infective larvae travel to the mouth of the mosquito. While the mosquito is feeding, the larvae are passed on to his host. The larvae will remain in the tissue for about two months. They then migrate to the right ventricle of the heart. In a period of approximately three and one-half months, the larvae will mature and begin passing microfilaria. Adult worms may live in the heart for years. As the worm numbers increase, they take up more and more space in the heart. This interferes with the normal function of the heart. If left untreated it will cause death.

Signs: Gradual weight loss. Lacking interest in activities normally enjoyed. Continuous cough. Coughing after being exercised, or falling down as if with a seizure.

Treatment: *Arsenamide* treatments over a three-week period are effective. The belief that the treatment will shorten the life of the dog is not true. It is the worm that causes the damage to the heart before and after treatment. Prevention is the best treatment. Preventive medicines may be given daily or monthly. Three chemicals have been found to be highly effective. Ivermectin (*Heartguard* - monthly), milbemyain (*Interceptor* - monthly) and diethylcarbamazine (*Filaribits* - daily) are the most popular choices.

In addition to preventing heartworm, these medications, in various forms, will protect against hookworm, roundworm, and whipworm.

CAUTION: Before giving your dog any type of heartworm medication, please have him examined by a veterinarian. Giving heartworm medication to a dog who has been infected with heartworm will kill him within 10 minutes. Some owners have resorted to the use of pure ivermectin. Ivermectin must be properly diluted and administered by body weight. Failure to dilute properly may cause ataxia, tremors, drooling, paresis, coma and death if overdosed. If underdosing occurs it may not be effective to prevent heartworms. In addition, plain ivermectin is not labeled to prevent hookworm and whipworm.

External Parasites

There are two types of mange that you should be aware of: sarcoptic and demodectic. Both types are caused by mites, so, when dealing with a true mange problem, you are dealing with mites.

Sarcoptic Mange

Sarcoptic mange is caused by parasitic mites. It is also highly contagious. The mite goes through four stages. All four stages are spent on the dog. It takes between 18 and 20 days to complete the life cycle. The female will burrow under the skin of its host to lay her eggs. The dog will scratch and chew at his body in an attempt to relieve the itching sensation caused by the burrowing mite. The dog will scratch so much that he will cause open sores to form. This scratching will cause a secondary infection. The secondary infection is usually much worse than the original problem and could cause death if untreated.

Signs: Continual scratching or chewing body; hair loss; dry, wrinkled skin. The mite may be detected from skin scrapings viewed under a microscope.

Treatment: Antiseborrheic shampoo or a shampoo containing sulfur. Ointments containing sulfur work well but tend to be greasy. Any good dip labeled for dogs will work just as well. Two to four treatments may be necessary depending on the severity.

Demodectic Mange

Demodetic mange, commonly called "red mange," is also caused by mites. It is not as contagious as sarcoptic mange, but it is much harder to destroy. This mite infests the hair follicle. The life cycle is between 20 and 35 days. Puppies become infected when nursing. All dogs may have this mite and are susceptible to it, but most have an immunity to some degree. This mange will usually make an appearance in a young dog, usually before he reaches one year of age. The symptoms may appear more rapidly when the dog has some type of physical or psychological stress. It is when the dog is fighting off the stress that the mite begins to win the battle.

Signs: Small hairless patches around the eyes, face or neck. Small pustules resembling human pimples may also appear. Even though remote and small when first noticed, they can spread over the entire body. Examining skin scrapings under a microscope is the only way to identify the demodetic mite.

Treatment: A topical application of *Amitraz* every two weeks until no live mites are found. If left untreated, secondary infections will complicate the condition and may cause death.

Fleas

Don't get excited—I don't have a miracle cure for the infestation of fleas. The flea, better known as a blood-sucking parasite, lives off the blood of its host. When the flea bites, it secretes an anticoagulant saliva. This enables the flea to feed freely. The flea will continue to feed even after it is full. This continual feeding stimulates the egg-laying process. The eggs are laid and fall off the dog and onto bedding, grass, carpet, etc. When the eggs hatch, the larvae feed off the blood-rich feces of the flea. When they emerge from the larval cocoons as adults, the cycle is completed. A flea can live up to two months without feeding. The flea will feed on humans, as well as animals. Fleas are also the carriers of tapeworms. Some dogs are allergic to flea bites. This allergy is usually described as dermatitis.

Signs: Missing hair around the areas of the neck, back or base of the tail. Hot spots. Black specs on the skin. If these specs turn red (actually blood) when placed on a wet paper towel, your dog has fleas. Even if there are no fleas visible, these black specs are flea feces and definitely indicate the presence of fleas.

Treatment: The only way I know to be rid of fleas is to treat everything simultaneously, including the dog, the doghouse, the dog's bedding, the yard and your home. The yard and the home may be treated with *Diazinon*, *Dursban*, or *Malathion 50*. Spray the yard every third day for nine days. This will insure killing the hatching eggs as well as the laying fleas. Keep your dogs off the sprayed areas until they have had a chance to dry. The dog should be washed and dipped. Washing and dipping should not reoccur for 14 to 21 days. This is not a permanent fix. It will have to be done every year around springtime.

CAUTION: Be extremely careful when spraying insecticides. They could be very toxic to your dog. Read all labels carefully and follow the directions explicitly. If there is no mention of dogs or fleas on the label, contact your veterinarian and ask for his advice.

Ticks

There are approximately 1500 different species of ticks that fall into five categories. These categories are: hard, leathery, poultry, reptiles, and soft. The information on these bloodsuckers take up 16 pages in the *Merck Veterinarian Manual*. Since there are so many of these parasites,

I will not attempt to describe them. The best that can be said is that they can cause great problems if proper action is not taken. Ticks can be found in tall grass, trees and just about any cool, damp area. They have a means of detecting the body temperature of the approaching host. A tick will generally attach itself to the neck and ear area of your dog. Check inside the ears as well as outside. Ticks seem to like the meaty portion of the interior ear. You may also find ticks in the soft areas of the legs, around the anus, the soft area of the genitals and on the tail. Occasionally, ticks will be found on the back or side of the dog. This does not occur very often. The best method for removing a tick is to use tweezers. Grasp the body of the tick firmly and apply a steady pulling pressure until the tick releases itself. Next, medicate the injured area with alcohol. If the head should break off and remain in the skin, it will usually become infected. This could cause secondary infection and other serious problems.

There is proof that several species of ticks transmit Lyme disease. Lyme disease may also be contracted by humans. The tick has to remain on its host for a period of 24 hours to pass on the disease. That is why it is so important to remove the tick as soon as possible. Also, severe tick infestation may cause anemia and death.

Anytime you or your dog are in an area where ticks may be found, check your dog and yourself thoroughly. Comb or brush your dog before putting him in his kennel or letting him in the house. Washing your dog with a flea and tick shampoo will help reduce the number of ticks your dog will attract. Be careful when washing your dog with these shampoos. Follow the directions on the label. Too much of the inert ingredients could be absorbed through the skin and cause your dog to have a negative reaction.

Ear Mites
The ear mite can also be a problem. The ear mite lives in the ear canal, sucking lymph glands by piercing the tender skin inside the ear. This will cause irritation, inflammation and the formation of a crust.

Signs: The dog will shake his head frequently. Scratching or rubbing his ears. A dark brown, waxy substance can be seen in the ears. In some cases there may be a noticeable odor coming from the ears.

Treatment: Hold the dog so he cannot shake his head. Place a few drops of hydrogen peroxide in the ear. Massage the base of the ear for approximately 15 seconds. Release the dog and allow him to shake this out. Repeat the same procedure for the other ear. Next, apply a miticide solution in each ear. Massage this in and hold the dog for as long as possible, so the miticide can do its job. This should be done every third day for four applications.

Prevention: Clean the dog's ears each time you clean the dog. Using alcohol to clean the ears periodically will remove water and keep the ears clean. This will help prevent bigger problems in the future.

Diseases

Rabies

Rabies is transmitted by means of saliva. The disease is passed on when an infected animal bites its victim. The infected animal does not necessarily have to be another dog. It could be any number of animals. If your dog is allowed to roam the woods, or, if you take him hiking and camping, he could come into contact with an infected animal. The disease can be passed on by means of inhalation. The disease can be present in the dog even if he is not showing any immediate signs of infection. The incubation period is between 15 and 50 days.

Signs: Change in behavior. Not eating or drinking. Seeking isolation. Frothing or drooling at the mouth.

Treatment: There is no treatment. The dog dies.

Prevention: The reason for a minimal amount of rabies in the United States is because dogs are vaccinated. Not getting your dog vaccinated is irresponsible and dangerous. This vaccine has been proven to prevent the spread of rabies in dogs. It is impossible to vaccinate all the animals in the wild. Because these animals in the wild cannot be vaccinated, rabies is still with us today. In addition to your dog being protected from the rabies virus, you lessen the chance of human infection. Rabies treatments for humans are available, but they are painful.

Distemper

Distemper is a highly contagious disease closely related to measles. The virus is sensitive to disinfectants and cannot live outside the body. There is a belief that this disease may cause multiple sclerosis in humans; however, there is no clinical proof of this.

Signs: High fever, runny nose, reddening of the eyes, and/or convulsions, depression, diarrhea. "Chewing-gum fits," or the chomping of teeth together, will cause excessive drooling. The dog will lie on his side with the legs moving as if running. The dog will have no control over normal body functions. Rear muscles will twitch or fail first. Blood tests will reveal a low white-blood count.

Treatment: Lots of fluids. Antibiotics to prevent secondary infection and to lower temperature. Nasal spray, anticonvulsant, and antibiotics. Keep the dog comfortable and calm. Most infected dogs will die.

Prevention: A series of vaccinations as a puppy with an annual booster vaccination.

Parvovirus

A very highly contagious disease, parvo is spread by the ingestion of fecal matter of infected animals. Dogs do not necessarily have to eat feces or urine to become infected. Since dogs seek out certain types of grass, it's possible for the matter to be on that grass. An infected dog may shed the virus for up to two weeks. The virus may remain viable for years. Although dogs of any age may acquire parvo, puppies between 8 and 12 weeks of age seem to be more susceptible. Incubation of the disease is from three to eight days. Signs may not appear for as many as seven or eight days. Death may occur within 24 hours after the first sign. Recovery may take from two to eight days.

Signs: Diarrhea containing blood, anorexia, and a rapid dehydration. Foul odor in feces. Some dogs may have a fever.

Treatment: Prompt, intensive care. Plenty of fluids and antibiotics. Intravenous fluid therapy is highly recommended.

Prevention: A series of vaccinations as a puppy with an annual booster vaccination.

Coronavirus

Coronavirus is also a very highly contagious disease. Although coronavirus is a different disease from parvovirus, it is similar in its symptoms. The treatment and prevention are the same as for parvovirus.

Hepatitus

There are two types of hepatitis. Both types attack the liver, kidney and the spleen. The disease is spread by urine, feces or saliva of infected dogs. The reactions vary from a slight fever to death. Young dogs are more at risk than older ones. The incubation period is from four to nine days. A high temperature will be observed for one to six days.

Six-month-old Abney's Patches with feline buddy Rocky.

Two good examples of healthy dogs.

Blair's Opal, a gray Leopard female, and Traxler's Chief, a blue Leopard male, playing on top of dirt mounds.

Signs: Apathy, anorexia, runny nose, watery eyes, and hemorrhaging. The clotting factor in the blood is the most affected. A small cut will bleed uncontrollably. Bleeding at the gum line.

Treatment: Daily blood transfusions. A very expensive process.

Prevention: A series of shots as a puppy and an annual booster.

Leptospirosis

This disease is spread by the common brown rat. Dogs of any age are at risk. Males appear to be affected the most. Incubation is 5-15 days. Death will occur within 5-10 days.

Signs: High temperature for several days, then a sudden drop. Labored breathing. Unquenchable thirst. Deep depression. Dog does not want to rise or move about. Sharp abdominal or back pain. Jaundice. Yellowing of gums and/or eyes. Blood test will reveal a high white-blood-cell count.

Treatment: *Tetracycline* and *streptomycin* medications. High doses of vitamin B. Intravenous feeding may be necessary. This, too, is a very expensive process.

Prevention: A series of vaccinations as a puppy and an annual booster.

Parainfluenza

Parainfluenza is another cause of kennel cough. This causes flu-like symptoms. Constant nagging cough, sneezing and watery eyes. This is not as serious a disease as the others mentioned, but it will open the door to secondary infection. Once in the kennel, it can cause havoc. If one dog is infected, it is recommended that all dogs be treated. This disease can be transmitted from one to the other and then back again.

Treatment: The treatment and prevention are the same. Once it is contracted, the dog will need a shot to clear up the problem.

Prevention: A series of vaccinations as a puppy and an annual booster.

After reading about all those shots and boosters, you're probably wondering how a dog can take all those shots. Parvovirus, coronavirus, distemper, hepatitis 1 & 2, parainfluenza, and leptospirosis have been manufactured so they can be administered in one shot. After a series of three shots at three-week intervals starting at six weeks of age, the dog may receive one annual booster shot. He will also need an annual rabies shot. Two shots a year to protect your pet. This is a lot less costly than having to treat one that is ill, or as painful as having to destroy him because of the lack of prevention.

General Information

Ears

The ears are usually the most overlooked part of the dog. Any dog that swims can get an infection from having water enter the ear. Dogs like the Catahoula, whose ears hang down, will tend to maintain a moist area, allowing bacteria to thrive. Bacterial and/or fungal infections in the ear canal are called otitis.

Signs: The dog will continuously shake his head in an attempt to rid himself of the irritation inside.

Treatment: Clean the dog's ears with a half-and-half mixture of alcohol and vinegar. Place a few drops of this solution in the dog's ears. Massage in gently from behind the ear, then clean them out with cotton balls. You cannot reach a dog's eardrums with you fingers because of the makeup of the dog's ears. Do not attempt to go any deeper than you can see.

Eyes

Dogs like to roll around in grass, sand and mud. During this action, the dog may get some debris in his eyes. This will irritate the eyes and, if not cared for, could cause a greater problem.

Signs: Rubbing at the eyes. A crusty buildup in the corners of the eyes. Reddening of the eyes, especially under the eyelid.

Treatment: Flush the eyes with an eyewash. This will help remove any debris that may be the cause of the irritation. Next, apply an antibiotic eye ointment. Be careful with this tube around the dog. If the dog should suddenly move, it could cause a more serious injury.

Teeth

A dog's teeth are his defense system and his only means of picking up things including food. You should check you dog's teeth regularly. Once a month you should brush his teeth and check for decaying teeth or any problems with the gums. If your dog will not let you brush his teeth, take him to your veterinarian. If the teeth are allowed to decay, it will cause health problems for your dog. If they are not cared for properly, the gums will suffer. Food will stick between the dog's teeth just like yours. You must help him get rid of this left-behind food.

Chew toys that allow a flossing effect are helpful, but you should have his teeth cleaned. This is just another way to add longevity to your pet's life.

Hot and Cold

Most people believe that the hair coat on the dog works the same as putting on an overcoat. This is not necessarily true. The hair coat on a dog is to protect the underlying skin from exposure and attack from airborne bacteria. The hair does act as an insulator to a degree, but it does not provide total protection.

Hyperthermia

This is overheating to the extreme. Joggers do not realize that exercise workouts for them may be killing their dog. Dogs want to please and will run until they drop. This is true with the working dog as well. On hot, humid days, if your dog is working, playing, or jogging with you, be sure to watch for signs of hyperthermia. A dog does not perspire like you do, so you must be aware of the signs. The tongue will hang very far out of the mouth and will widen. There may be some saliva dripping off the tongue. This is the radiator system of dogs. They perspire from the mouth and the pads of their feet. This is the only method they have to keep cool. This is the time to stop the activity and seek a cooler place. To cool the dog, have him lie down. Place a cool cloth under the pits of the forelegs. Wipe the head and back of the neck with a cool cloth. Give the dog lots of water and a liquid containing some form of electrolyte. Some sports drinks have electrolytes in them. Consult your veterinarian as to the amount you should administer.

Hypothermia

This is the opposite of hyperthermia. The dog will get cold and the same problems exist. The dog will seek a place out of the wind and cold and curl up into a ball. That hair is for protection and is not an overcoat. Get the dog warmed up. Cover him with a blanket or some other object of warmth. Both heating and cooling the dog should be done slowly. If it is done too rapidly, it will cause the dog to go into shock.

Both of these symptoms can kill a dog if you are not aware of what is happening to him. Enjoy your dog, but remember, he cannot tell you when he is sick, tired or sore. You will have to observe your friend. Be alert for signs of stress or fatigue. A good master will do this on a daily basis.

Lagniappe

Pronounced "lan-yap" it is a word used in Louisiana to mean "a little extra." There are three major points that have increased the life span of dogs. They are:

1. Control of infection and disease through the use of vaccines.
2. Heartworm prevention.
3. Automobile death prevention. Both those run over by cars and those left in closed cars.

Two major points to save new born pups are:

1. Heat source. Keep your puppies warm. Prevent them from getting chilled.
2. Give sugar water if they become chilled or sick. Mix one teaspoon of honey to 8 ounces of water. Give 1ml orally every 30 minutes to prevent dehydration. Pediatric electrolytes may also be used. Administer 1ml every 30 minutes. Do not dilute.

Two major points for geriatric pets are:

1. Obesity. Weigh your dog once a month to help control your dog's weight.
2. Keep the dogs' teeth clean. Remove those that are decayed. Decayed teeth will poison a dog's health system.

Chapter 9

BREEDING AND GENETICS

Almost everything you read concerning dog breeding will tell you that you shouldn't breed dogs because there are already too many in the world. You will read that there are not enough people to provide homes for them. What these articles fail to tell you is that the dog lovers of the world are in the minority. I know you don't understand how anyone couldn't absolutely love these wonderful animals. They don't, and that's their loss; however, these books are correct. There are too many dogs for the number of dog lovers. So why do people continue to breed them?

Some breed to improve the hunting prowess of their dogs. Some are trying to develop a new breed. Some want their children to experience the wonders of birth. Some believe they can make a lot of money. Some are totally irresponsible and can't figure out how their dogs got pregnant. Then there are those who breed to better their bloodlines while knowing that the entire litter may have to remain with them. Still others breed to keep up their working stock of dogs.

These may seem like good or bad reasons, but they are all true. So, where do we stand on this breeding issue? That's a decision you'll have to make. Since almost everyone has read these articles and continues to breed anyway, I feel that I should try to explain what you are up against if you are going to breed Catahoulas.

Before you start any action in the breeding process and before the dogs are old enough to breed, you must check your dog's background. Knowing the bloodlines and the genetics in your particular lineage should help in making a decision whether to breed your particular pair of dogs.

The reasons for this research are to find out if there are problems with the eyes, hips, joints, teeth, jaw, bone structure and skull development and to determine if there is any predominant deafness, blindness, sterility, or aggressiveness anywhere along the bloodline. I say predominant because it is possible to have one pup from any litter that may possess these deficiencies. If there are three or more pups in a litter with any or all of these problems, I would look for another dog for breeding purposes. It is possible for one dog in a bloodline to possess the genes that are causing these problems. This does not mean that the entire bloodline is bad. If this trait runs true in most of the dogs in that bloodline, then I would look for another bloodline. Know your bloodlines and any genetic problems before you do anything else.

Investigate the lineages of any dogs you use from outside your bloodlines as well. This does not guarantee that your bloodline will be problem free, but it will reduce the risk. You will want to guarantee your puppies just as you expected a guarantee when you acquired your dogs.

You should understand what breeding is all about before you breed any dogs. You can place any male and female dog together and get puppies, but this does not make you a breeder. Knowing and understanding the breeding systems are just as important as the purchase of the dog you intend to breed. There are inbreeding, linebreeding and outcrossing systems. There are rotational and topcrossing programs contained within these systems. There are books available that will explain these practices in great detail.

Inbreeding, which is considered to be the taboo by most individuals not familiar with breeding procedures is the mating of mother to son, father to daughter, or full brothers and sisters from any litters involving the same parents.

The classic five-color Catahoula.

Abney's Cocoa—a chocolate Catahoula with amber eyes.

Linebreeding, which is a milder form of inbreeding and considered to be the safest way of maintaining a bloodline is the mating of grandfather to granddaughter, grandmother to grandson, aunt to nephew, uncle to niece or half brothers and sisters from any litters involving either parent.

Outcrossing, which is the breeding of any two dogs that are not related to each other in any way. Some breeders feel that continuous outcrossing will eventually produce a mongrel, or a dog without a definite bloodline. This would make it almost impossible to identify any inherited problems.

From this brief explanation you can see the importance of knowing and understanding the different breeding procedures and why they are used.

None of these procedures are bad if they are used properly and intelligently. You should know these systems and understand why you are using the program you chose. You should also learn as much as you can about genes and what an important part they play in any breeding program. You must thoroughly understand what you are doing before you embark on this project.

There are many good books on breeding and genetics available at a reasonable cost. I advise you to obtain a few of them before getting involved in breeding.

Deafness is the greatest problem in the Catahoula. Amidst the Catahoula genes is the M locus. This is commonly called the merle gene. It's the one that causes that colorful coat, those unusual eyes, deafness, blindness and sterility. What can you do? Not much at this time. Check the bloodlines and ask about the problems within them. Generally, the dogs with predominantly white coats, over 60 percent white, are going to have problems with deafness, blindness or sterility. There is also a probability that these dogs will pass them down the line. Also, dogs with an all-white face and blue eyes will be deaf or partially deaf about 80 percent of the time.

What do you do with a deaf or blind puppy? You will have to put him down—euthanasia. I would never knowingly let a defective puppy leave the kennel. I know there are deaf dogs and blind dogs that are doing just fine out there in the world, but these are the exceptions and not the rule. Destroying a puppy can be a very difficult thing to do, but consider the consequences of keeping him. A mature dog who is deaf or blind could seriously hurt someone just by reacting instinctively.

When a dog is deaf he relies heavily on his instincts. If you startle this sleeping dog, his instinct will be to protect himself. What does he use? TEETH! SHARP TEETH! Imagine a small child waking a deaf dog to play. The dog will not hear the child coming and will be startled from his sleep. The results could be disastrous. There is also the chance that you may see him run over by a car, because he didn't hear the horn. Wouldn't you rather humanely destroy a defective puppy?

Dr. George Strain, Ph.D., Director of Veterinarian Medicine at Louisiana State University has been working on the deaf problems occurring in Dalmatians. These are the same problems the Catahoula is having with deafness. I have personally donated deaf puppies to his program to isolate the problem and maybe someday prevent it from happening.

There are tests that can be performed on the puppy to determine deafness when he is 14 days old. These are simple tests that send audible clicks at varying frequencies and do not harm the puppy in any way. The results are printed through a computer program that helps determine if the puppy is deaf. This is the surest way to tell.

Dr. Strain, professor of Neuroscience, Louisiana State University, School of Veterinary Medicine, has provided the following information:

> Deafness in dogs, which can affect one or both ears, can be congenital or acquired later in life. Congenital deafness, which actually develops during the third week of life, is frequently inherited, and is usually a result of the genes responsible for coat color. Acquired deafness may be a result of age, infection, trauma, drug or other chemical toxicity, or noise (i.e., gun fire). Acquired deafness may be partial or complete, and may affect one or both ears. Dogs with acquired deafness generally fare well, but may be at risk for vehicular death if allowed to run free. Their disability will not be passed on through breeding.
>
> Congenital deafness occurs in a variety of breed (over 45) and with a surprising frequency. The actual incidence of congenital deafness in Catahoulas is unknown; incidence

can be quite high, based on studies in other species, such as the Dalmatian, where unilaterally and bilaterally affected animals reach 30 percent. Dogs deaf in both ears are usually detected within weeks: they sleep through feedings after weaning and do not waken in response to loud noises, but early detection is often missed because they cue off of the behavior of litter mates. Dogs deaf in just one ear are frequently never detected unless specialized testing methods are employed: the only behavioral clue for these dogs is difficulty in localizing sound sources and they usually adapt quickly. They may perform poorly as working dogs but they make acceptable pets. However, if bred they may produce additional deaf offspring. Generally, deafness is complete for each affected ear.

Deafness results soon after birth because blood vessels in the cochlea degenerate, resulting in the death of the hair cells that the nervous system uses to detect sound. The blood vessels are though to die as a result of the absence of pigment cells (their function is not known). Thus, the deafness is actually the result of a pigment fault, and may be associated with visible pigment indicators in the hair coat and iris. Two coat pigmentation genes are associated with most congenital deafness: the merle gene (seen in the Catahoula, Collie, Shetland Sheepdog, and Old English Sheepdog, among others) and the piebald gene (Bull Terrier, Dalmatian, English Setter). In breeds carrying the merle gene, such as the Catahoula, deafness is increasingly likely to be present with increasing amounts of white in the hair coat, and with the presence of one or two blue irises, where the blue is the absence of normal iris pigment. The merle gene is autosomal dominant, but the deafness associated with the gene is not necessarily inherited by the same mechanism. Only future studies will enable a determination of the mechanism of inheritance of this genetic defect. Dogs deaf in one ear have the defect, but it is expressed in the one ear. As a result, when bred these dogs may have an increased chance of producing deaf offspring.

Diagnosis of deafness by subjective methods, either by the breeder or veterinarian, relies on detecting a behavioral response to an unseen noise (hand clap, jingle of keys). Hearing puppies often tire of the game and quit responding, while deaf puppies may detect movement or vibrator clues, falsely indicating hearing ability. The results, especially for dogs with unilateral deafness, are very unreliable. Unequivocal diagnosis requires use of the brainstem auditory evoked response (BAER), a specialized test usually available at schools of veterinary medicine and a few specialty veterinary practices. In this test a computer records the electrical response of the auditory system to click stimuli from scalp electrodes; when the response for one ear is absent the ear is deaf.

Dealing with bilaterally deaf puppies presents a quandary. They can be considerably more difficult to raise than hearing puppies, and often die from vehicular causes if allowed to run free. They may bite when startled, so they may not be safe around young children. Abnormal personalities may develop because of being repeatedly startled. In general, it is advised that these puppies be euthanized. Because this is emotionally difficult to do after placement of puppies, hearing assessment should be performed by the breeder before homes are found.

What is the BAER test? The hearing test known as the brainstem auditory evoked response (BAER) or brainstem auditory evoked potential (BAEP) detects electrical activity in the cochlea and auditory pathways in the brain in much the same was that an antenna detects radio or TV signals or an EKG detects electrical activity of the heart. The response waveform consists of a series of peaks numbered with Roman numerals: peak I is produced by the cochlea and later peaks are produced within the brain. The response from an ear that is deaf is an essentially flat line. In the sample recordings shown below, Puppy 1 heard in both ears, Puppy 2 was deaf in the left ear, Puppy 3 was deaf in the right ear, and Puppy 4 was deaf in both ears. Because the response amplitude is so small it is necessary to average the responses to multiple stimuli (clicks) to unmask them from the other unrelated electrical activity that is also present on the scalp (EEG, muscle activity, etc.).

The response is collected with a special computer through extremely small electrodes placed under the skin of the scalp: one in front of each ear, one at the top of the head, and one between and behind the eyes. It is rare for a dog to show any evidence of pain from the placement of the electrodes—if anything the dog objects to the gentle restraint and the irritation of wires hanging in front of its face. The stimulus click produced by the computer is directed in the ear with a foam insert earphone. Each ear is tested individually, and the test usually is complete in 10-15 minutes. Sedation or anesthesia are usually not necessary unless the dog becomes extremely agitated, which can usually be avoided with patient and gentle handling. A printout of the test result, showing the actual recorded waveform, is provided at the end of the procedure. Test results are confidential, but anonymous details will be used in Dr. Strain's ongoing deafness research for later publication and education of veterinary practitioners.

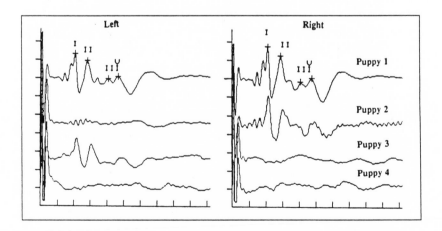

When breeding Catahoulas, the general rule to follow is, if the female is light-colored, breed to a medium- or dark-colored dog. If the female is dark-colored, breed to a medium- or light-colored dog. Breeding two light-colored dogs will give you a lighter-colored litter, and you run an even greater risk of deafness, blindness or sterility. If you breed two dark-colored dogs, you will probably get an all dark litter, mostly solid black. Breeding two medium-colored dogs is all right. This does not guarantee there will not be any deaf puppies, but it does reduce the chances of its happening. We can breed beautiful animals but not without some degree of risk or responsibility.

You should have homes for your puppies before you breed. I know this sounds like an impossible thing to do, but this is how I run my kennel. I will let people know when I expect the next heat and what male I will be using. I will skip the mating if there are not at least eight people waiting for a puppy. I chose the number eight, because experience has shown that at the time of a request these people wanted a dog from this kennel. Either they grew tired of waiting and found a litter that was available elsewhere, or they just got another breed of dog entirely. I am a little disappointed when this happens, but I feel that, if they could not wait, the puppy is better off going where he is wanted. This is also better for the Catahoula breed, because those people who change breeds in the waiting process really didn't know what they wanted.

Now that you have all your background work done and you are sure you have a perfect pair and a waiting list, you're ready to start breeding. You should also consult your veterinarian for books that deal with the breeding of dogs. The process is the same for most dogs.

One thing to keep in mind is that a champion does not necessarily produce champions, and the opposite is also true. Your dog does not have to be a champion to produce champions. I know of a pair who were bred and their entire litter became champions. The very next time they were bred, the entire litter was a disaster. I pass this on to you so you will be prepared.

Always try to stay as close to the standard as possible. No matter how pretty the other dog is, if he or she doesn't fit the standard the puppies probably won't either.

The female should not be less than 12 months old. The male should be approximately 14 months old. These are the ideal ages for the reproductive systems to be fully functional. Some larger dogs may require a little longer to mature. You should never use a male that does not have both testicles.

Your female should be wormed and checked by your veterinarian before she is bred. She will also need to be checked during the pregnancy and again about one week after whelping. Visiting the veterinarian in advance will enable him to be familiar with your dog in case there are any problems with the pregnancy or the delivery. While at your veterinarian's office, ask for the emergency telephone number. Problems seem to occur when the doctor is not in the office.

The general rule of thumb for a female in heat is: seven days coming, seven days in, seven days out. There will also be a noticeable swelling of the vulva. The female going into heat will generally have a light discharge. This is sometimes hard to notice, since most females are

Two litters from the same breeding pair produce different colors.

Aden's Honey Bunch with her puppies at lunch time.

continually cleaning. The next stage is the bleeding. This usually starts at about the third day. The length of time the bleeding will last varies with each female.

There are five days when the female is most fertile and will generally become pregnant. This is the 10th through the 14th days.

I will generally breed twice during this time using the following method: days 10 and 12, or days 11 and 13, or days 12 and 14. Since the discharge is not always easy to see, I count seven days from the first spotting of blood and then introduce the female to the male once on each of the breeding periods. The reasons for skipping a day are to allow the male to build up his sperm and give him some rest.

A sure way to tell if your female is ready is to watch her and the male. They will go through a ritual of playing, running and jumping together before any action occurs. When the female is ready, she will raise her tail and hold it over to one side. We call this "flagging." When her flag is up, she is ready. The male knows this instinctively and will do the necessary deed.

While we are on this subject, let's talk about accidental breeding. I often hear people say: "She was in her own yard and this male from down the way came in and got her pregnant before I knew what was happening!" Oh, really! Didn't they know their female was in heat? A female in heat gives off a scent. This scent can be detected by a male up to one mile away. If the female is giving off the signals, the males are going to visit.

I understand that an accident can happen, but you must be prepared to stop the breeding process if you don't want puppies. To give you an idea of what to expect, let me tell you a story.

My kennel is set up with concrete runs and six-foot high fencing. The houses are arranged outside of the runs with a hole cut through the wire so the dogs have access to the inside of the houses. There is a five-foot overhang made of fiberglass panels so the dogs can get out of the sunlight and heat. When I had a female go into heat, I felt that she was okay and nothing could happen. Well, it did!

She climbed over the gate and circled the kennel yard. She then climbed up on top of one of the houses and jumped to the roof of the overhang. Being fiberglass, it didn't hold her weight. She crashed through the roof and into the pen with a male. Yes, she bred even after the six-foot fall. Luckily, she chose the same male I had chosen and didn't break any bones in the fall. Now I have a wire top that I place over the pen when a female goes into heat. No one in—no one out. This way the decision to breed is mine.

During the mating, the dogs may assume what is called the "tie." When this happens, both the male and the female will place a strain on each other while waiting to separate. If you have an aggressive female, you will want to hold her still so she does not seriously injure the male. The mating pair do not have to tie for the breeding to be successful. In most cases, if the tie occurs, there is a successful breeding.

A Catahoula requires about 63 days before whelping. A pregnant female needs good food and exercise. Let her exercise the way she did before she became pregnant. Forty days from the breeding she should not be allowed to jump up, on or off anything. Jumping up requires the use of rear legs and stomach muscles. This places pressure in the stomach area and could cause problems with the puppies. Jumping down will cause a jolting sensation and also cause problems. Do not allow her to play with other dogs at this time. Dogs playing together tend to bump into one another. This also could cause problems. These are just a few precautions that should be taken.

Before your litter arrives, you will want to arrange a clean, dry, warm place for the female and the pups to stay. Puppies cannot be allowed to get a chill, or it will kill them. A puppy cannot shiver until it is about three weeks old. If he cannot shiver, his only way to keep warm is by being close to the mother or having an external heat source.

When the whelping begins, keep an eye on the female and make sure she isn't having any problems. It is not necessary for you to stay during the entire delivery. I find that staying around makes the female nervous. She becomes concerned about your being there, which adds to her ordeal. Just check on her and make sure she is okay. Once the first puppy arrives, she will have her pups about one hour apart. She may rest between puppies. If you should see a puppy being delivered backwards or breached, it's okay. This doesn't make any difference.

When all the puppies are delivered, I will let the whelping female and her puppies have the next three days to get accustomed to each other and the new surroundings. I check in on them, but I will not handle them unless it is necessary for their safety. I feel that the puppies just got dropped into new surroundings and need time to adjust. After the third day, I begin handling the pups and will continue to handle them until they leave. This is part of socializing them. It gets them used to humans and being touched.

When the puppies are three weeks old, you should prepare a place where the female can isolate herself from the puppies. Closing off a section of your whelping yard with a 16-inch high partition will suffice. This way the puppies cannot get to her but she has access to them. You do not want to stop the female from nursing her puppies, but she will begin getting sore from the sharp teeth and claws and will need a place to rest away from the puppies.

I have my whelping pen set up so the female can reach the puppies by jumping from one yard, her sanctuary, to the whelping yard. I accomplished this by placing a gate in the dividing fence and leaving a 16-inch high removable section of fencing in place under the gate. This

Two litters from the same breeding pair. Note the difference in colors between the two litters.

way I do not have to worry about whether the pups are annoying the female or if the pups are being fed. The female knows that when she is full, the pups need to nurse to reduce the supply. This makes it easier for all concerned. When the female is moved back to her housing pen, I will take out the removable panel under the gate allowing the puppies to utilize both pens. This gives them plenty of room to play.

Puppies should begin eating solid food at three weeks of age. Do not feed the puppies and the whelping female in the same area. The whelping female should be fed separate from the puppies to reduce the competition for the food. Start by mixing solid food with a milk re-placer. The way I handle the first week of feeding is to pulverize food in a food processor. This will make a powder of the food. I then mix this powder with the milk replacer and let it stand until it is soft. Make the first feeding very soupy. Take each puppy one at a time and intro-duce him to the mixture. I find the easiest way to do this is to hold the puppy at the edge of the dish with one hand and place some food on a finger of the other hand. Next, place the finger covered with food close to the puppy's mouth. When he starts to suck at it, move your hand to the dish slowly. He will follow your hand down to the dish. From that point on, the puppy will eat his fill. This feeding should be done at least twice a day, although some prefer three feedings. The second week of feeding solid food, I use the small chunks from the bag and add milk replacer. Let it stand until soft and give this to the puppies. Don't despair if they do not eat it all. It's different from what they have become accustomed to, and they may leave some. Give it to the whelping female. Do not save it. By the time they are between five and six weeks old, they will be eating dry food. It's really that easy. Even though the puppies are eating solid food, they should still be allowed to nurse. Since the puppies are now getting full bellies without nursing, the whelping female will gradually reduce her supply of milk.

I do not wean my puppies. I allow the female to decide when she is not feeding any longer. Generally, the pups will be eating solid food and only nursing occasionally when they leave the kennel. This is between six and eight weeks of age. As a puppy leaves, there is less demand for milk. The female senses this and reduces the supply.

When the pups are six weeks of age, I will remove the female from the whelping yard and only allow her to nurse occasionally until all the pups are gone, or when she stops producing milk. I find that this slow reduction enables the female to recover much quicker and does not place any burden on her. It also reduces the chances of her getting mastitis.

The puppies will need to be wormed at two, three and five weeks of age. The whelping female should also be wormed at the two- and three-week mark. All the puppies should get their first vaccination at six weeks of age.

You should be prepared to keep the puppies until they are eight weeks old. This is the amount of time a puppy needs to be with his litter mates. It is during this time that they learn the pecking order and the whelping female gives instructions in behavior.

Your litter papers should be filled out when the puppies are two weeks old. Fill in the areas that make reference to the male's lineage. The papers must be signed by the owners of both breeding dogs and sent along with the payment of the litter registration. You will receive your puppy papers about three weeks after filing. This will enable you to have all the documentation to give to your clients at the time of sale.

I try to impress on any new breeder that your female may come into heat every six months, but she should not be bred in each heat cycle. I like to breed in one cycle and skip the next. If I breed the same female in two cycles back-to-back, I will not breed her in her next heat. I feel that she needs the rest and the time to build up her system. It also gives your female a longer life and helps produce consistent numbers in your litters.

I hope I've helped you understand the undertaking of breeding Catahoulas. This may seem like a lot to learn, but remember, you are going to be creating life. When it doesn't turn out like you expect, you'll be asking yourself: "What am I going to do with all these puppies?"

If you can't sell them, you could give them away. Let me give you the scenario of what generally takes place with most puppies that are given away.

To start with, the puppy did not cost the new owner anything. No investment, no loss. Time will be spent with the puppy while he is growing up, but puppies lose that delightful play and innocence and begin to investigate different surroundings. This could involve chewing shoes, clothes, furniture, etc. He could also begin digging holes or eating plants or just being a nuisance. If the new owner does not spend time training the dog, he could become a real problem to them. Unless this person really cares about the dog, he will not receive the obedience training necessary to avoid problems. Their next step might be to take him to the pound.

That may solve the immediate problem, but someone else may end up with this dog who is now totally confused and cannot distinguish right from wrong. Then, again, he may be put to sleep.

You could have brought this dog to the pound yourself, but why breed dogs if you are not ready to keep them or have an avenue to place them in loving homes. If you take puppies to the pound, don't complain that your tax dollars are being thrown away because of unwanted pets you helped create.

You could take a drive into the country and dump them in the woods. Most people believe that with this exposure they will go back to the wild and take care of themselves. Sorry, but a puppy in the wild becomes a part of the food chain. If he does survive, it is highly possible he will mate with a coyote and create what farmers call a "coy-dog." This half-coyote and half-dog will kill livestock and has no fear of man. This results in higher costs of food for consumers, or, if there is someone who is responsible for getting rid of these renegade animals, you are spending your tax dollars again. Even if the dogs don't become food for other animals and do make it in the wild, eventually you will see them lying alongside a highway.

If you are going to breed to get rich, STOP. When you add up the cost of the veterinarian office visits, food, shots, three wormings, advertising and the time it takes to accomplish all this, it will cost more than you make. Your chances of getting rich are better with the lottery.

If you are breeding so that your children can experience the wonders of birth, buy a tape or watch a nature show on the educational channel.

There is no truth to the saying that a female should have a litter of puppies before she is spayed. A female will mature whether she has a litter or not. Proof in point. What about a sterile female? Doesn't she mature? And without a litter? The same holds true for a male. He does not have to father a litter before being neutered. I don't know where these stories came from, but they are not true. Spaying or neutering may change a dog's personality, but it will not enhance maturity.

If you never tasted ice cream, you would never want any. The same thing is true for the dog that never has a litter or fathers one. THINK ABOUT IT.

You find Catahoulas in the strangest places.

Chapter 10

In Conclusion

As you can see, the undertaking of a Catahoula can be fun, rewarding and useful. These are some of the finest dogs I have ever been in contact with. They are loving, loyal, protective and at times a real pain in the neck. They will try your patience just as a child would. They will attempt to be the boss, and, if you let them, you will have a great deal of trouble reclaiming that position. If you succeed, you and your dog may not have that mutual respect that was formed when you first bonded.

The key is to stay in charge without being cruel or breaking the dog's spirit. Obedience classes will achieve this, but you must work with your dog's routine weekly.

If you have decided to become a breeder, read the chapter on breeding again. It is important that you understand what needs to take place when breeding.

The biggest problem in the dog world is the breed that becomes popular for a time. I refer to this as the "Yuppie dog."

Yuppie dog means that the breed is a fad and popularity will eventually fade.The problem is when a dog is popular it will demand a higher price. Unscrupulous breeders and individuals see this as a get-rich-quick venture. They are the uncaring puppy-mill breeders and the owners that just don't care about the breed—only the money. Yes, money will be made but at the expense of the breed. Bloodlines aren't checked, and defective genetic traits are ignored. The result of this is the breed will get a bad reputation. It is not the fault of the dog but rather that of the owner or breeder.

What I have described to you is what has happened to many of the breeds described as vicious dogs. These vicious breeds are not really vicious. There may be one or two that must be culled, but, for the most part, these are good dogs. It's the owners who create the problems. True breeders are concerned with their particular breed and will try to improve on that breed by not making the mistakes of happenstance breeding. Time and patience are important in this undertaking.

A good breeder knows that these dogs will need to be cared for daily by having their water changed regularly, daily feedings and their pens cleaned. Time must be spent with each dog. He must be allowed to get

"Hey, where's the ball?" Four-month-old chocolate, blue and gray Leopard littermates.

exercise, whether it is raining or the sun is shining, whether it is hot or cold, or whether or not you had a bad day at the office. You must be the same person with your dogs each time you make contact with them. This is sometimes the hardest thing for humans to do. We find it hard to be the same with each other, let alone our animals.

Dogs have a way of knowing your feelings just by being around you. They will try to make you happy by doing their best to please you. They are always glad to see you, no matter what. They don't care if you are clean or dirty, smell bad or sweet, or are pretty or ugly. A dog will give you unconditional love. All it asks in return is for a pat on the head and a hello.

Dogs are used by hunters to track game.

Dogs are used by police departments to help fight crime.

Dogs are used by farmers and ranchers to assist with chores.

Dogs are used to locate lost and missing persons.

Dogs are used as therapy for persons in nursing homes.

Dogs are used by the handicapped to do the routine things we take for granted.

Dogs provide us with entertainment.

In some areas dogs are used as a means of transportation.

What a sad place this world would be without our dogs.

Balentine's Shadow taking a nap between shows.

Bibliography

AKC Book of Dogs, The.

Atlas of Dogs, The. Wilcox/Walkowicz.

Catahoula Collection, The. Mrs. J. S. (Betty Ann) Eaves.

Civilization of the American Indian, The. Thomas Page.

Grolier Collegiate Encyclopedia.

Historic Indian Tribes of Louisiana. Fred B. Kniffen, Hiram F. Gregory, George A. Stokes.

History of Choctaw, Chickasaw and Natchez Indians. H.B. Cushman.

History of Louisiana. Charles Gayarre.

Indian Tribes of the Lower Mississippi Valley and Adjacent Coast of the Gulf of Mexico. John Reed Swanton.

Inheritance of Coat Color in Dogs. Clarence C. Little, Sc.D.

Louisiana Historical Quarterly. Louisiana Historical Society Cabildo, New Orleans LA.

Pictorial History of the American Indian, A. Oliver LaFarge.

Simon & Schuster's Guide to Dogs. Gino Pugnetti.

For Additional Reading from Doral Books, see:

Winning With Pure Bred Dogs: Success by Design, by Dr. Alvin Grossman and Beverly Grossman.

The Standard Book of Dog Breeding: A New Look, by Dr. Alvin Grossman.

Fido, Come! Training Your Dog With Love and Understanding, by Liz Palika.

General Canine Glossary

Afterbirth: The placenta attached to the sac in which puppy is born.

All-Breed Club: A club devoted to the showing and breeding of purebred dogs. Membership is open to breeders and exhibitors of all breeds. Holds championship shows.

Arbiters: Dog-show judges.

Artificial Insemination: Impregnating a bitch with frozen or extended sperm.

Awkward Phase: Rapid-growth period for a puppy usually associated with plaining out of the head features. Occurs from three to eight months.

Back: That portion of the topline starting just behind the withers and ending where the croup and loin join.

Backcrossing: To cross a first generation hybrid with one of the parents.

Balance: Overall fitting of the various parts of the dog to give a picture of symmetry and correct interaction.

Best In Show: Top award in an all-breed show.

Best Of Winners: Defeats other sex winner. Captures that sex's points if greater than its own on that day.

Bitch: A female dog.

Bite: Position of upper and lower teeth in relation to each other. Various breed standards call for different kinds of bite often based on function.

Bloodline: A specific strain or type within a breed.

Bottle Feeding: Using a doll bottle to feed formula to a newborn puppy.

Breaking Point: Limit to what the dog can endure.

Breech Presentation: Puppy born feet first rather than head first. Can cause whelping difficulties as puppy may get turned sideways in the birth canal.

Brucellosis: A sexually transmitted disease or infection.

Bulbus Glandis: A portion of the penis closest to the testicles that fills with blood to three times its size during the sexual act. It serves to "tie" the male and female together while the male ejaculates sperm.

Caesarean Section: Removing puppies from the womb surgically.

Campaigning A Dog: Seriously exhibiting a champion to compete for top honors.

Canine Herpes Virus: An infection in puppies caused by an infected dam. A leading cause of puppy mortality.

Canine Parvovirus: Myocardial forms attack only puppies. Severe, often fatal reaction. Cardial form attacks older dogs.

Chromosome: Cell nucleus of all multicell organisms that contain DNA. Comprising the genes of that species.

Colostrum: A part of the bitch's milk that provides puppies immunity from many viral and bacterial diseases.

Contour: Silhouette or profile, form or shape.

Conformation: The form and structure of the various parts to fit a standard.

Crate: A metal, plastic or wood kennel (in various sizes). Dogs may sleep and travel in them.

Cryptorchid: A male dog with neither testicle descended.

Dam: Mother of a litter of puppies.

Degeneration: Used in reference to inbreeding. After primary generations, stock shows reduction in size, bone and vigor.

Dehydration: Loss of body fluids—may lead to death.

Developmental Phases: Stages through which puppies grow.

Dew Claws: Hardy nails above pastern. Most breeds have them removed. In many breeds they are not present.

DNA: Deoxyribonucleic acid genes. They are regarded as the building blocks of life.

Dominant: Color or characteristic that covers up all others that are recessive to it.

Eclampsia: An attack of convulsions during and after pregnancy.

Egg: A female reproductive cell.

Estrus: Period of bitch's heat cycle when she is ready to breed.

Exhibitors: People who show their dogs.

Expression: Facial aspect or countenance.

Fallopian Tubes: Conduits for eggs from ovary to uterus.

Fetus: The growing puppy within the womb.

Filial Regression: The tendency of offspring to regress toward mediocrity if controlled breeding is not carried out.

Fluid Pressure: Pressure caused by pumping action of the heart as the blood flows through the veins and arteries.

Forechest: The point of the thorax that protrudes beyond the point of the shoulder.

Foreface: That part of the muzzle from just below the forehead to the nose.

Gene: The smallest unit of hereditary information.

Genetics: The study of the science of heredity.

Genotype: Genetic term meaning the unseen genetic makeup of the dog.

Gestation: The organic development of the puppy within the uterus.

Gravity: The pull of the earth upon a body.

Groom: To comb, clip and brush a dog.

Handler: Person showing the dog.

Handler's Apprentice: A person learning the handler's trade.

Heat: A bitch coming into season so she can be bred. Usually twice a year.

Heredity: The sum of what a dog inherits from preceding generations.

Hetrozygous: Non-dominant for a trait or color. Carries both dominant and recessive genes for a variety of traits.

Homozygous: Dominant for a trait or color. Carries no recessive for that characteristic.

Hybrid: Dogs who have gene pairs — non-dominant.

Hybrid Vigor: The extra vigor or development exhibited by offspring of an outcross.

Hyperthermia: A chilling of the puppies which is liable to cause death.

Inbreeding: Very close familial breeding, i.e., brother X sister, father X daughter or son X mother.

Inguinal Ring: Muscles of the abdominal cavity (groin) that prevent adult testes from going back up into abdominal cavity and, which can prevent their proper descent in puppies.

Judge: A person approved by association to judge dogs

Kinetic Energy: Relating to the motion of bodies and the forces and energy associated therewith.

Labor: The act of attempting to whelp puppies.

Lead: A strap or cord fastened around dog's neck to guide him. Also called leash.

Lead Training: Teaching the dog to walk and trot properly so as to best exhibit his conformation. May also be used for control.

Line Breeding: Breeding closely within a family of dogs, i.e., grandfather to granddaughter.

Malnutrition: Lacking the proper nourishment to provide normal healthy growth.

Metritis: A uterine infection in the dam that can transmit bacterial infection to an entire litter.

Monorchid: A male dog with only one testicle descended.

Monstrosities: Severe, often lethal deviations from expected structure, usually brought out through inbreeding.

Natural Selection: Charles Darwin's theory of how species evolve.

Neonatal: New born.

Neonatal Septecemia: An infection in newborn puppies picked up by staphylococcus germs in the dam's vaginal tract.

Non-Dominant: An animal with characteristics that are mostly recessive.

Nucleus: The center of a cell. Contains chromosomes and is essential to all cell functions, such as cell division for reproduction.

Outcrossing: Matings of animals that are somewhat inbred to unrelated animals to reinstate vigor and substance.

Ovulation: The female process of creating eggs for reproduction.

Ovum: An egg ready for sperm to fertilize it.

Parasites: Infestations of lice, ticks or fleas as well as internal infestation of various worms.

Pastern: The body's shock absorber. Located at the juncture where the paw meets foreleg.

Pedigree: Hierarchical listing of ancestors.

Phenotype: The actual outward appearance as can be seen—opposite of genotype.

Placenta: A vascular organ that links the fetus to the dam's uterus. Nourishes and mediates fetal change. Also known as an afterbirth.

Plaining Out: Usually occurs as head changes because of the loss of puppy teeth.

Postpartum: After birth.

Pounding: Results when front stride is shorter than rear. Hindquarter thrust forces front feet to strike the ground before they are fully prepared to absorb shock.

Pregnant: Term used for bitch carrying puppies.

Producing Power: The ability to stamp one's get with positive features of championship caliber.

Proestrus: First part of heat cycle.

Professional Handler: A person paid to show and train dogs.

Profile: Outline or silhouette.

Proportion: Relationship, ratio of one body part to another.

Proven Sire: Male dog that has enough offspring to judge his potency.

Puppy Septicemia: Bacterial infection caused by a mastitis infection in the dam. Often fatal if not treated immediately.

Purebred: A dog whose sire and dam are of the same breed and whose lineage is unmixed with any other breed.

Quarantine: A period in which a dog is isolated from other animals while being observed for communicable diseases.

Recessive: Color or trait which is not dominant and must link up with another recessive for expression.

Ribs: The thorasic vertebrae that surround the heart and lungs.

Sac: Membrane housing puppy within uterus.

Scrotum: Housing for male dogs testicles.

Showmanship: The bravura exhibition of a dog.

Sire: Father of a litter.

Spermatozoa: Motile sperm from male dog.

Standard: An official description of the breed developed by breed's parent club.

Structural Design: The blueprint from which the originators of a breed sought to create a dog for the task at hand.

Subcutaneous Muscle: That type of muscle which lies directly under the skin.

Symmetry: A pleasing balance of all parts.

Test Breeding: A mating usually of a parent of unknown genotype and one of a known genotype to reveal what characteristics the unknown one will throw.

Tie: The locking together of the dog and bitch during mating caused by the swelling of the Bulbis Glandis just behind the penis bone.

Topline: That portion of the dog's outline from the withers to the set on of the tail.

Toxic Milk Syndrome: Toxic bacteria in dam's milk having a toxic effect on nursing puppies.

Type: Characteristics distinguishing a breed.

Unbroken Line: A pedigree line of continuous producers down to the current sire or dam.

Umbilical cord: A cord that connects the fetus with the placenta attaching at the puppy's navel.

Vaccinations: Shots administered to ward off certain diseases.

Vulva: External parts (lips) of bitch's genital organs.

Wean: Gradually changing puppies to solid food away from mother's milk.

Whelping Box: Where you wish to have the litter born and the bitch doesn't. Used later for nursing bitch and her puppies.

Withers: Highest point on the shoulder blades.

Index